G000075552

THE
BRAVEST
DEEDS
OF
MEN

A FIELD GUIDE FOR THE
BATTLE OF BELLEAU WOOD

Colonel William T. Anderson, USMCR (Ret)

History Division
United States Marine Corps
Quantico, Virginia

2018

This pamphlet history, one in a series devoted to U.S. Marines in the First World War, is published for the education and training of Marines by the History Division, Marine Corps University, Quantico, Virginia, as part of the Marine Corps' observance of the centennial anniversary of that war. Editorial costs have been defrayed in part by contributions from members of the Marine Corps Heritage Foundation.

No. 4 in the U.S. Marines in World War I Commemorative Series

Acting Director of Marine Corps History
Paul J. Weber

WWI Commemorative Series Historian
Annette D. Amerman

WWI Commemorative Series Editor
Angela J. Anderson

CONTENTS

FOREWORD

The Battle of Belleau Wood in June 1918 was the first major engagement between the Germans and U.S. Marines. The Germans were stunned to find that not only could the Marines fight, but they were also deadly marksman who were incapable of quitting the field of battle until it was theirs. Today, *Bois de la Brigade de Marine* and the surrounding woods, small towns, and farmland appear much the same as it did a century ago. The battlefield remains scarred with the impact craters from artillery and the trenches and defensive positions carved into the ground by a previous generation of fighters. With the creation of Colonel William T. Anderson's, USMCR (Ret) field guide, visitors can now walk the area with the history of the battle in their pockets and at their fingertips. This guide was written based on Colonel Anderson's experience leading staff rides and private tours of the battlefield and will give readers the ability to experience the terrain on their own.

Colonel Anderson led Marines on tours of Belleau Wood for 10 years while stationed at Supreme Headquarters Allied Powers Europe in Belgium. He served as the officer-in-charge, Reserve Augmentation Unit and Deputy Chief of Staff, Headquarters Marine Corps Forces Europe, from 1992 to 1998. From 2009 to 2017, he served on the adjunct faculty of the Command and Staff College's Distance Education Program, Marine Corps University, Quantico, Virginia. He has published numerous articles and notes about Belleau Wood in the course of his career. This field guide serves as an excellent addition to our U.S. Marines in World War I Commemorative Series and as a useful tool for Marines, historians, and all those interested in the battle.

Paul J. Weber
Acting Director
Marine Corps History Division

PREFACE

In a series of battles in France in World War I, the U.S. 2d Division fought for control of an area called *Bois de Belleau* (Belleau Wood) near the town of Château-Thierry. It was here in this former hunting preserve that the 4th Brigade won fame and glory. In commemoration of the deeds and sacrifices of those who fought here, the French Army commander renamed the Bois de Belleau as *Bois de la Brigade de Marine* or the Marine Brigade Wood.

The words and deeds of Marines during this battle have become important parts of Marine Corps history and tradition. Indeed, some aspects have become Marine Corps legend. For example, the origin of the nickname "Devil Dogs" is said to have its roots in Belleau Wood. Legend states that the Germans were so impressed with the aggressiveness of the Marines that the soldiers called the Marines Devil Dogs after the large hunting dogs that victimized them at the nearby Château Belleau. In fact, the term from which Devil Dogs is derived—*Teufelhund*—is possibly a creation of the Marine Corps' own Publicity Bureau as it was used on an April 1918 recruiting poster. More significantly, besides its strategic and operational consequences in blunting the German offensive and restoring hope to the exhausted Allies, the fighting at Belleau Wood is generally considered to be an evolutionary bridge in the development of the modern and "Always Ready" Marine Corps of today.

The origins of this field guide began in the early 1990s with a group of Marine Corps officers serving with the author at the North Atlantic Treaty Organization's (NATO) Supreme Headquarters Allied Powers Europe (SHAPE) in Casteau, Belgium. Recognizing the importance of Belleau Wood to Marine Corps history, the Marines at SHAPE would drive to Belleau Wood and attend the Memorial Day and Veterans Day ceremonies at the Aisne-Marne American Cemetery and Memorial in Belleau, France, adjacent to Belleau Wood. It was during this period that informal battlefield walks started in 1992. Colonel Larry K. Brown (Ret), Colonel John H. Turner (Ret), and Lieutenant Colonel Edward T. Forte (Ret) contributed to this effort.

Following the establishment of the U.S. Marine Corps Forces Europe (MARFOREUR) headquarters in Stuttgart, Germany, in 1993, more Marines in Europe were able to attend the annual Memorial Day ceremonies at the Belleau cemetery. Believing it important for Marines attending these ceremonies to take advantage of the opportunity to learn more about the battle, the author and Lieutenant Colonel Thomas W. Williams at MARFOREUR worked on an organized battlefield tour. They approached then-Brigadier General David Mize, deputy J-3 (operations) at U.S. European Command (EUCOM), with the idea of a formal staff ride. Until this time, an organized group study of Belleau Wood had never been done. With Mize's guidance, they developed an appropriate staff ride that was conducted in 1995. Under the leadership of then-Brigadier General Michael W. Hagee (later 33d Commandant of the Marine Corps), who became deputy J-3 at EUCOM in 1996, the original battlefield tour was expanded into a full-day battle study on the Saturday prior to the annual Memorial Day ceremonies. Marines who contributed to this effort also include General Robert B. Neller, Colonel M. C. O'Neal (Ret), Lieutenant Colonel W. E. Holdorf (Ret), and Lieutenant Colonel E. M. Velasquez (Ret). Their efforts live on in these pages. That original staff ride, with its stands at historically significant locations, is the foundation of this publication and uncounted battlefield tours for Marines since that time.

The author feels particularly fortunate to have been able to collaborate with Lieutenant Colonel R. L. "Bill" Cody, who produced the remarkable maps. This was truly a working relationship as they challenged each other on several occasions to ensure the maps were not only accurate but also an effective complement to the text. Cody's artistic talent and technical ability allowed him to create these excellent maps that contribute significantly to the overall result. The battle maps presented in this guide are based on maps published by American, German, and French authorities after the war. The base maps for the stands in the itinerary section came from recent satellite images of the battlefield. What is fascinating is the fact that the terrain and vegetation has changed very little in the last 100 years.

The author is very grateful for Cody's assistance and friendship. Generous financial assistance for this project came from the Marine Corps Heritage Foundation. The grant allowed the author to continue the research and travel associated with the project.

There is one final acknowledgment. Gilles Lagin of Marigny-en-Orxois, France, continues to be a valuable source of information about the countryside around Belleau Wood and the movements of American soldiers and Marines during the battle. His passion about all things associated with the Marine Corps in the Great War is remarkable and noteworthy.

The title of this guide comes from the Edgar A. Guest poem, "Battle of Belleau Wood," published in 1922. It was reportedly General John A. Lejeune's favorite poem of all the verses written after the war.

Battle of Belleau Wood

It was thick with Prussian troopers, it was foul with German guns;
Every tree that cast a shadow was a sheltering place for Huns.
Death was guarding every roadway, death was watching every field,
And behind each rise of terrain was a rapid-fire concealed
But Uncle Sam's Marines had orders: "Drive the Boche from where they're hid.
For the honor of Old Glory, take the woods!" and so they did.

I fancy none will tell it as the story should be told—
None will ever do full justice to those Yankee troopers bold.
How they crawled upon their stomachs through the fields of golden wheat
With the bullets spitting at them in that awful battle heat.
It's a tale too big for writing; it's beyond the voice or pen,
But it glows among the splendor of the bravest deeds of men.

It's recorded as a battle, but I fancy it will live,
As the brightest gem of courage human struggles have to give.

Inch by inch, they crawled to victory toward the flaming
  mounts of guns;
Inch by inch, they crawled to grapple with the barricad-
  ed Huns
On through fields that death was sweeping with a mur-
  derous fire, they went
Till the Teuton line was vanquished and the German
  strength was spent.

Ebbed and flowed the tides of battle as they've seldom
  done before;
Slowly, surely, moved the Yankees against all the odds
  of war.
For the honor of the fallen, for the glory of the dead,
The living line of courage kept the faith and moved
  ahead.
They'd been ordered not to falter, and when night came
  on they stood
With Old Glory proudly flying o'er the trees of Belleau
  Wood.[1]

Are you ready to join us "through the wheat"?

---

[1] This and many other similar writings can be found in their entirety in W. D. Eaton, ed., *Great Poems of the World War* (Chicago: T. S. Denison, 1922), 29–30.

ESTABLISHMENT OF THE 4TH BRIGADE

Activation of Marine Corps Units

Although America's participation in the Great War began officially on 6 April 1917 with the declaration of war, the secretary of the Navy, Josephus Daniels, anticipated dramatic increases in requirements for the naval Service. With the Naval Act of 1916 (Public Law 64-231, dated 29 August 1916), both the Navy and the Marine Corps expanded dramatically. Supported by Secretary of the Navy Daniels, Major General Commandant George Barnett concluded he could provide two regiments of Marines for service with the American Expeditionary Forces (AEF).

The first of these, the 5th Regiment, was hastily organized from existing companies at various posts, stations, and ship detachments throughout the Marine Corps with an activation date of 8 June 1917. By order of President Woodrow Wilson, the regiment was transferred to control of the War Department, which was responsible for the AEF vice the Navy Department. This new regiment was among the first AEF contingents to go to France, with the 1st Battalion arriving on 27 June 1917. The second, the 6th Regiment, began assembling at Quantico, Virginia, the new Marine Corps base, on 11 July 1917.

After considerable pressure for the use of the Marines, the War Department authorized a brigade of Marines on 20 September 1917 to replace an Army brigade originally planned for the Army's 2d Division. Joining the 5th Regiment, the battalions of the 6th Regiment arrived in France on 5 October 1917. On 23 October 1917, the brigade was organized formally, consisting of the 5th Regiment and elements of the 6th Regiment, plus units of a machine gun battalion still embarked, with newly promoted Brigadier General Charles A. Doyen, commander of this new 4th Brigade. Doyen opened the 2d Division headquarters on 26 October 1917. On 8 November 1917, he turned over command of the division to Army Major General Omar Bundy.

The Marine Corps formed a machine gun battalion on 17 August 1917, consisting of the 77th and 81st Companies for service with the regiments. When the 5th Regiment left for France, each of its battalions included a machine gun company. Later, as the Marine battalions arrived in France, the machine gun companies were reorganized into the 6th Machine Gun Battalion with four companies (15th, 23d, 77th, and 81st) to support the brigade. In addition, each Marine regiment contained one machine gun company: 5th Regiment (8th Machine Gun Company) and 6th Regiment (73d Machine Gun Company). By 28 December 1917, the reorganization was completed and the 6th Machine Gun Battalion joined the brigade.

Since coming to France, the Marines had performed mostly stevedoring and guard duties. According to many accounts, it was a dreary experience for the Marines. With the coming of the New Year, activity picked up and training began in earnest. On 12 January 1918, Colonel Albertus W.

Catlin opened 6th Regiment headquarters. With the arrival of the 2d Battalion on 5 February 1918, the regiment was now intact. Major Holland M. Smith served as the brigade adjutant or operations officer.[2] When Doyen returned to the United States in early May due to illness, Army Brigadier General James G. Harbord, formerly the AEF chief of staff, became the new brigade commander.[3]

The 2d Division went to the trenches on 13 March 1918 in a so-called "quiet sector" southeast of Verdun, France, for frontline training. From 17 to 30 March, these elements participated in the occupation of sectors on the west face of the Saint-Mihiel salient. The division continued its service at the front until 13 May, when it was relieved to conduct further training. On 18 May, it was assigned to the French Group of Armées of Reserve. As a result of the German offensive on 27 May 1918, the brigade's scheduled Decoration Day (now known as Memorial Day) festivities were canceled. The division was placed at the disposal of the French Sixth Army on 31 May and directed to the French XXI Corps sector near Château-Thierry to assist in the Aisne defensive, which put the Marines on the road to Belleau Wood. The rest, as they say, is history.

---

[2] Gen Holland Smith (1882–1967) entered the Marine Corps in 1905. Transferred to the I Corps, First Army, in July 1918, he served as assistant operations officer in charge of liaison during the Aisne-Marne, Oisne-Aisne, Saint-Mihiel, and Meuse-Argonne offensives. After the Armistice, he participated in the march to the Rhine through Belgium and Luxembourg as an assistant operations officer with the Third Army, and served with the General Staff, U.S. Army, during the occupation of Germany. Sometimes called "the father of modern U.S. amphibious warfare," he was one of America's top commanders in the Pacific during World War II. Most notably, he led Task Force 56 (Expeditionary Troops) at Iwo Jima, which included all the assault troops in that battle. The three Marine divisions were commanded by former lieutenants who had fought at Belleau Wood: MajGen Keller E. Rockey (5th Marine Division), MajGen Graves B. Erskine (3d Marine Division), and MajGen Clifton B. Cates (4th Marine Division).

[3] Gen Harbord (1866–1947) would later command the 2d Division and end the war leading the American Expeditionary Forces's Services of Supply, transforming its operations into a model of efficiency.

Devil Dogs in Navy Blue and Gold

At the same time the Marine Corps experienced significant growth for the war in Europe, the U.S. Navy expanded the Chaplain Corps and the Medical Corps to support the new requirements.

U.S. Navy Chaplain Corps: although the Navy's Chaplain Corps had been serving aboard ships for many years, only one chaplain was assigned to the Marine Corps in 1917. Chaplain Edmund A. Brodmann had been serving at Marine Barracks Port Royal, South Carolina, since 19 November 1916. According to the Chaplain Corps' history: "His tour of duty marks the beginning of the unbroken connection of Navy chaplains with the Marine Corps."

Subsequently, Chaplains George L. Bayard and John J. Brady joined the 5th Regiment in Philadelphia, while the regiment waited to sail to France in June 1917. Later, Chaplains James D. MacNair and Harris A. Darche were directed to Quantico to join the newly forming 6th Regiment and were with the regiment when it arrived in France late in October 1917. As the 4th Brigade formed, each regiment had one Roman Catholic and one Protestant chaplain. Additional chaplains arrived with the replacement battalions throughout the remainder of the war. Ultimately, 13 chaplains served the Marines in France, participating in every major engagement. Four chaplains were awarded the Navy Cross for their actions and were the first chaplains so honored: Chaplains Brady, Darche, MacNair, and Albert N. Park, who had replaced Chaplain Bayard.

Chaplain Brady's exploits at Belleau Wood are representative of the exemplary conduct of these brave men of the church providing religious services to their Marines. His Navy Cross citation reads:

The President of the United States of America takes

pleasure in presenting the Navy Cross to Lieutenant, Junior Grade (Chaplain) John J. Brady, United States Navy, for extraordinary heroism in the line of his profession in serving with the Fifth Regiment (Marines), 2d Division, American Expeditionary Forces. Chaplain Brady exposed himself fearlessly, making a complete tour of the front lines twice, and carrying cigarettes to men who would not have had an opportunity otherwise to get them. He carried out his duties as a Chaplain with devotion and was cool under fire.

Throughout the war, the Navy chaplains served with distinction under difficult circumstances by either providing comfort or support to those on the front line or by being present at the aid stations to minister to the wounded and dying.

U.S. Navy Medical Corps: medical officers have served with the U.S. Navy since the dawn of the Republic. However, it was not until 1842 that a Navy Bureau of Medicine and Surgery (BUMED) was established to formalize selection and training. Following the national catastrophe of the Civil War and concerns about medical care on the battlefield, the Medical Corps was created as a separate entity within the Navy in 1871. With the expansion of naval commitments at the end of the nineteenth century, Navy medicine entered a "brilliant chapter" of professionalism, culminating with the creation of the Hospital Corps for enlisted personnel on 17 June 1898. Supporting the fleet surgeons, these medical sailors have been referred to as "hospital corpsmen" ever since.

In addition to expanding the Marine Corps, the Naval Act of 1916 resulted in a dramatic increase and reorganization of the Navy's medical organization to include the Hospital Corps. Although hospital corpsmen had served with distinction with the Marine Corps prior to 1917, the transition of the Marine Corps from expeditionary operations to a prolonged land campaign required a change in focus for medical support. Gone were the simple days of a routine sick call. Modern war demanded medical personnel embedded with tactical units responsible for battlefield casualties. The history of Navy medical support to the Marines in the war shows that initially each regiment had 7 medical officers, 3 dental surgeons, and 48 hospital corpsmen. Medical personnel were generally distributed as follows with each regiment:

Regimental aid station:
    Senior medical officer (surgeon)
    Assistant medical officer
    Senior dental officer (dental surgeon)
    Chief pharmacist's mate
    Hospital corpsmen (6–8)
Battalion aid station:
    Surgeon
    Assistant surgeon
    Dental surgeon (if possible)
    Chief pharmacist's mate
    Hospital corpsmen (5–7)
Each company:
    Hospital corpsmen (2–4)

After the brigade's first casualties in the frontline trenches, it became clear that having five corpsmen per company was better with one man assigned to each platoon with four platoons per company. In addition, when there were enough personnel, a second or first class pharmacist's mate was assigned to each company to supervise and assist the corpsmen. A typical battalion medical unit is portrayed in figure 1.

As is routine procedure today, initial medical care is

Figure 1. Medical Unit, 3d Battalion, 6th Regiment.
Bureau of Medicine and Surgery, Navy Department

a personal responsibility. Intervention by trained medical personnel is necessary when wounds are more severe, and so it was with the 4th Brigade in 1918. Medical personnel entered combat with their units and provided first aid on the battlefield. If required, they arranged for transport to the nearest battalion aid station. Battalion aid stations were located as close to the action as was prudent, usually 0.5–2 kilometers, and acted as triage centers treating minor wounds and directing more seriously wounded personnel to the rear by ambulance for treatment at an appropriate field hospital.

This close relationship with mobile warfare is now taken for granted but was an entirely new concept in naval service in 1917. The approximately 300 Navy medical personnel who served with the 4th Brigade during the war took care of their Marines in every combat operation. Treating more than 13,000 casualties, Medical Corps sailors suffered their share of casualties with 18 killed in action and 165 gas casualties.

A heritage of valor and brotherhood was born in the bloody fields of France. Of the four Medals of Honor awarded at Belleau Wood, Navy medical personnel received two: Navy doctor Lieutenant Orlando H. Petty and posthumously to dentist Lieutenant (Junior Grade) Weedon E. Osborne.[4] The Navy Medical Corps was awarded a total of six such prestigious medals during the war. Other sailors earned a host of awards for heroism, including the Navy Cross, the Army's Distinguished Service Cross, and the Silver Star Medal.

The conduct of Pharmacist's Mate Second Class Frank G. Welty on 6 June 1918 typifies the selfless devotion to duty Marines have come to expect from their corpsmen. He was attached to the 20th Company, 3d Battalion, 5th Regiment, as it assaulted Belleau Wood on that fateful day. As the battalion crossed the wheat field, the devastating machine gun fire caused terrible casualties. According to the account recorded by Navy Lieutenant George G. Strott, Hospital Corps, Welty was "swamped with many wounded while in the open field." However, he cared for the Marines as best he could until he was mortally wounded. As he lay dying, he gave his book of diagnosis tags to his patient with instructions to "turn them over to the chief" at the aid station. Welty was awarded a Distinguished Army Cross for his devotion to duty at his final hour. Later, his family received a Navy Cross from the Navy for the same act. The award of a medal for valor by both Services for one action was a practice followed in other cases in the war, as the Navy Cross was first authorized in 1919 and awarded to many Navy and Marine Corps veterans of World War I.

---

[4] Petty (1874–1932) was originally from Harrison, OH, and entered the Navy in 1916. After the war, Dr. Petty returned to Philadelphia, where he taught at the University of Pennsylvania Graduate School of Medicine, served as the head of Philadelphia's public health department, and headed the Bureau of Communicable Diseases. Osborne (1893–1918) grew up on a combined working farm, school, and orphanage for boys in Allendale Farm, Lake Villa, IL. He graduated from Northwestern University Dental School in 1915 and was appointed a dental surgeon in the U.S. Naval Coast Defense Reserve on 8 May 1917. Osborne served at the Boston Navy Yard and on board the USS *Alabama* (BB 8) before he transferred to the 6th Regiment in France on 26 March 1918.

Another example can be seen in Navy Commander Paul T. Dessez (1876–1940), Medical Corps, regimental surgeon, 5th Regiment, recipient of both the Distinguished Service Cross and Navy Cross. Colonel Albertus Catlin, the 6th Regiment commander at the time, noted in his post war memoir:

> *Surgeon PAUL T. DESSEZ, U. S. N.,*
> *Regimental Surgeon, 5th [Regiment]:*
> *On the day that the regiment suffered its heaviest losses, June 6, 1918, this officer organized the service of caring for and evacuating of the wounded in a most systematic and admirable manner. As there were few of his officers and men who had had experience in this work and as the terrain and the villages in which the above work was organized were not well known, the duty required almost constant exposure to the fire of the enemy on the part of Surgeon DESSEZ; it is felt that to the extraordinary heroism, coolness and energy on his part, was due the efficiency with which this work was performed.*

The former commander of 2d Battalion, 6th Regiment, General Thomas Holcomb, concluded after the war:[5]

> *The naval medical personnel who served in the Fourth Marine Brigade . . . acquitted themselves with exemplary honor. They won for their corps and branch of service a record of war accomplishment ranking high in naval history.*

---

[5] Gen Holcomb (1879–1965) was the 17th Commandant of the Marine Corps. He commanded the 2d Battalion from August 1917 and served as second in command of the 6th Regiment, taking part in the Aisne defensive (Château-Thierry), the Aisne-Marne offensive (Soissons), actions in the Marbache sector, the Saint-Mihiel offensive, the Meuse-Argonne (Champagne) offensive, the Meuse-Argonne (Argonne Forest) offensive, and the march to the Rhine in Germany following the Armistice. In recognition of his distinguished service in France, he was awarded the Navy Cross, the Silver Star with three oak leaf clusters, a Meritorious Service Citation by the commander in chief, AEF, the Purple Heart, and was cited three times in General Orders of the 2d Division.

This special relationship would endure throughout the war and continues to the present day.

Devil Dogs in Olive Drab

2d Engineers, U.S. Army: the 2d Division also included the Army's 2d Engineer Regiment. As the division deployed to the vicinity of Château-Thierry, the commander directed that the engineer regiment support the two infantry brigades by assigning a battalion to each brigade—the 4th Brigade and the 3d Brigade (9th and 23d Infantry Regiments). Once the battle for Belleau Wood began in earnest, however, the two engineer battalions would come to reinforce the two Marine regiments. Although the engineers were sent forward to "consolidate positions" (i.e., digging in), the soldiers eventually served as combat replacements due to the considerable casualties in the Marine battalions. With shovels and their 1903 Springfield rifles, the Army engineers fought side by side with the Marines throughout the desperate struggle. As highlighted in the Spring 2003 *Army History* magazine article on the regiment's service at Belleau Wood, with the glory came the sacrifice:

> *During the period 1 June to 16 July 1918, when it was employed at Belleau Wood, the 2d Engineers suffered 452 casualties, losing 91 killed in action, 30 dying of wounds, and 331 wounded. With an assigned strength of 1,697, it had in this period endured a casualty rate of 26.7 percent!*

This sacrifice earned the regiment an honor of considerable value: the admiration and respect of the 4th Brigade. Colonel John W. Thomason Jr., in his classic 1928 book *Fix Bayonets!*, wrote:

> *There was [sic] always good feelings between the Marines of the 2d Division and the Regular Army units that*

formed it, but the Marines and the 2d Engineers—"Say.
If I ever got a drink, a 2d Engineer can have half of it!"—
Boy, they dig trenches and mend roads all night, and
they fight all day!

U.S. Army Infantry Officers in the Brigade: as the nation prepared for war, the U.S. Army decided to expand its divisions from three infantry regiments to four, which were organized in two brigades. Additionally, each infantry battalion increased from three to four companies, resulting in a need for company officers of the lower grades. In the Marine Corps, providing additional units to form two Marine regiments resulted in a shortfall of junior officers as platoon leaders for what was to become the 4th Brigade. Although many qualified Marine Corps noncommissioned officers were commissioned, the number of qualified individuals was limited and did not support the significant increase demanded by the war effort. The deficit was made up by assigning junior officers from the Army to the Marine Corps.

Once the 4th Brigade was formed in France and began training in earnest, nearly 60 U.S. Army officers were made available for service with the Marines and joined the brigade prior to Belleau Wood. Many remained with the brigade through Soissons in mid-July 1918. Others, possibly replacements, went on to serve with Marines at Saint-Mihiel, Blanc Mont, and in the Meuse River campaign. Thirteen Army officers were killed or died of wounds during the war while serving with the Marines.

One exceptional soldier was First Lieutenant Elliott D. Cooke (1891–1961) of the 18th and later the 55th Company, both in the 2d Battalion, 5th Regiment. An enlisted soldier who was commissioned in 1917, Cooke wrote an excellent memoir of the war for the *Infantry Journal* in 1937. Cooke was highly thought of by the battalion commander,

Lieutenant Colonel Frederic M. Wise. When Captain John Blanchfield, the 55th Company commander, was mortally wounded on 7 June, Wise gave Cooke command of the battalion. As the battalion assaulted Belleau Wood on 11 June, Cooke led his company superbly, later receiving three Silver Star Citations. The awards' citations note that he, the sole survivor of the company officers, rallied his men with extraordinary skill and heroism and continued to lead them forward. Cooke remained in command of the company through mid-July at Soissons.

U.S. Army Medical Support: in addition to infantry and engineers, the brigade also was supported by U.S. Army medical and dental personnel. These soldiers either served with the Marine units or were responsible for wounded once they left a regimental aid station for further treatment in the rear. If the wounded needed significant medical care beyond that available at a regimental aid station, members of one of the 2d Division's 2d Sanitary Train's four ambulance companies transported the casualties toward the field hospitals (figure 2). There were four Army Medical Corps field hospitals taking care of the 2d Division: Field Hospitals 1, 15, 16, and 23. Field Hospital 1 served as the farthest forward triage site in Bezu-le-Guery. Field Hospitals 15 and 23 were full surgical units for "nontransportable" wounded. Field Hospital 16 was for the gassed and sick. Field Hospital 23 was located at La Ferté-sous-Jouarre and Field Hospitals 16 and 15 were both at Luzancy.

Initially, the Army medical staff remained part of the division's 2d Sanitary Train, but they were then attached to the battalions as required. For example, figure 1 shows First Lieutenant John D. Southworth (1890–1972), fourth from right, second row. This doctor from Ohio was a member of the 15th Ambulance Company. He attended Kenyon Military

Figure 2. Evacuation of Marine casualties,
Montreuil, France, 8 June 1918.
Official U.S. Army, Medical Department photo

Academy in Ohio, a preparatory academy for Kenyon College, from which he graduated in 1911. Southworth enlisted in the Ohio National Guard in the spring of 1917 while a medical student at Johns Hopkins University in Baltimore, Maryland. He deployed to France in 1917 after finishing his third year and subsequently was awarded his medical degree and commissioned in the Army Medical Corps on 28 May 1918. Dr. Southworth was awarded a Silver Star for meritorious conduct under fire at Blanc Mont and a French Croix de Guerre.

Throughout the 4th Brigade during the battle, Navy corpsmen mingled with soldiers from the ambulance companies. On 2 June 1918, a detachment from the 23d Ambulance Company was sent for duty as litter-bearers and first aid men with both the 5th and 6th Regiments. One particular soldier from the 15th Ambulance Company attached to the 5th Regiment exhibited exceptional courage on 6 June 1918. Army

Private Louis H. Harkenrider received the Distinguished Service Cross for actions described in the following citation:

On June 6, 1918, in the vicinity of Chateau-Thierry . . . he went out into an open field under heavy shell and machine-gun fire and succeeded in bandaging and carrying back to our lines a wounded comrade.

Unfortunately, many Marines would require such care in June 1918. The remarkable servicemembers of the 2d Sanitary Train were not without casualties. An early Army casualty was Private First Class Herman Goetz, an ambulance orderly, who was killed by artillery fire on 6 June at the 6th Marines' Regimental Aid Station at Montgivrault Farm. The very next day, five soldiers attached to the 6th Regiment were gassed and had to be evacuated.

THE BATTLE
OF BELLEAU WOOD

The Situation

In the spring of 1918, Germany held an excellent position to inflict a decisive blow on the western front. Russia's withdrawal from the war enabled Germany to transfer more than a million experienced soldiers and more than 3,000 guns to the west. Now, for the first time, Kaiser Wilhelm II's army had numerical superiority. Equally important though was the sad state of the Allies—the French were exhausted after four years of war, the British Army had sustained serious losses at Ypres in Flanders, and the Italians had been thrown back at Caporetto. Even so, Germany's main hope of victory depended on early successes before the Americans could reach the front in large numbers.

However, the German High Command underestimated its new opponent. First, the Americans transported their troops across the Atlantic in convoys escorted by the British Navy far faster and in greater numbers than the Germans believed possible. By 1 March 1918, the month the German offensive began, there were more than 290,000 American troops in France. By October, the number swelled to 1.7 million. Second, these troops were more combat ready than Germany anticipated.

Nevertheless, on 21 March 1918, Germany began their final offensive, hoping to gain a decisive victory. Conceived by General Erich von Ludendorff, the plan involved the destruction of the British Army in the north to be followed by a crushing blow against the French in the south. The initial German offensive was clearly a victory but only a tactical success. In a battle known as the Second Battle of the Somme, the Germans failed to destroy the British for the most part because the Germans lacked ample reserves at each front to exploit local breakthroughs. After a week, both sides were exhausted. Then, on 8 April 1918, the Germans renewed the offensive against the British. This attack, known as the Battle of the Lys, involved a massive artillery bombardment followed by overwhelming infantry attacks that swept the British back. As in the first offensive, French reserves played a key role in denying complete victory to the Germans. However, the use of the French reserves in support of the British left the French sector lightly manned.

On 27 May 1918, the Germans launched another attack —the Third Battle of the Aisne—but this time against the French and British units between Soissons and Reims (map 1). This move caught the Allies by surprise and, within four days, the Germans stood on the banks of the Marne River. Assaulting across a 48-kilometer front, they drove over the Chemin des Dames ridge and quickly exceeded the German High Command's expectations.

On 29 May, they captured the important railroad junction of Soissons and began to exploit their success, getting ever closer to Paris. The result was the demoralization of the Allies and several bulges or salients in the Allied line. Ev-

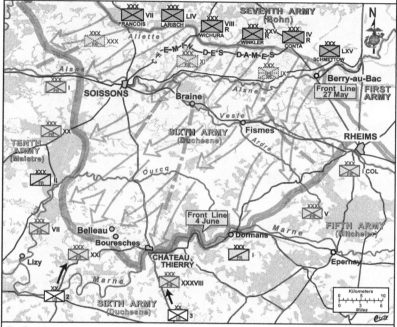

THE GERMAN SPRING OFFENSIVE, 1918
Operation Blucher, 27 May–4 June
In May 1918, the Germans secretly massed six corps (totaling 29 divisions) in the *Seventh Army (Bohn)* sector along the Allette River north of the Chemin des Dames. On 27 May, the *Seventh Army* attacked, overwhelming the defending French Sixth Army (Duchesne) consisting of two French and one British corps (a total of 11 divisions).

The French rushed reserves forward to contain the German advance, finally holding the enemy in a huge salient that extended in the north from Soissons to Reims and south to Château-Thierry on the Marne River. The U.S. 2d Division (including the 4th Brigade) was attached to XXI Corps and the 3d Division to XXXVIII Corps of the French Sixth Army (Dochesnes). Facing them were the battle-tested divisions of the German *IV Reserve Corps (Conta)*. The stage was set for the legendary clash of arms in the first major battles fought by Americans in WWI.

Map 1. Germans launch their spring offensive.
Map by LtCol R. L. "Bill" Cody, USMC (Ret)

erything played out in Germany's favor; however, with the speed of the advance, they had outrun their logistics and exhausted the troops (figure 3).

The French were in a panic and the government prepared to abandon Paris, which now sat only 48 kilometers from the front. Although the Allies were in disarray, there was one unknown variable: the Americans. Army General

Figure 3. The German advance, May 1918.
American Battle Monuments Commission

John J. Pershing, the American commander, had initially been adamant that his soldiers would fight together as an American Army. However, due to the emergency situation, he reluctantly agreed to assign U.S. divisions to the French Army (figure 4). Thrown into the battle piecemeal within the French sector where they could do the most good, the Americans proved themselves to be worthy opponents. The Americans were blooded when the 1st Infantry Division fought valiantly at Cantigny on 28 May; and the 3d Infantry Division (forever after known as the "Rock of the Marne" division) prevented the Germans from crossing the Marne River at Château-Thierry on 31 May 1918.

At the same time, despite early confusion due to conflicting orders, the 2d Division deployed east toward Château-Thierry via truck convoys. In an ironic twist, the trucks were driven by French colonials from an area in Indo-China now known as Vietnam. After a difficult trip against waves of fleeing refugees, the Marines arrived at Montreuil-aux-Lions, east of Paris, on 1 June. Disembarking, the troops marched about 8 kilometers along the

Figure 4. Marine deployment to Château-Thierry.
American Battle Monuments Commission

Paris-Metz road. It appears that, purely by chance, the 4th Brigade was tasked to defend an area north of the Metz road, northwest of Château-Thierry, in the vicinity of Lucy-le-Bocage. This decision would direct the Marines toward their destiny at Belleau Wood.

BATTLE
CHRONOLOGY

What follows is a chronological narrative for the Battle of Belleau Wood. It is not intended as a comprehensive account of the battle but an introduction. Several references in the bibliography are more detailed and should be consulted if interested.

27 May 1918
A major German offensive begins between Soissons and Reims. Referred to as *Corps Conta*, after its commander, General Richard Heinrich von Conta, the *IV Reserve Corps*, *7th Army*, attacks toward Château-Thierry.[6]

30 May 1918
The 2d Division Headquarters, near Chaumont-en-Vexin approximately 56 kilometers north of Paris, is alerted to prepare to move north that evening due to the emergency. Confusion within the Allied command reigns as the 2d Divi-

---

[6] Richard Heinrich Karl von Conta (1856–1941).

sion's deployment changes direction. *Corps Conta* advances with the *10th Division*, *36th Division*, and *28th Division* (right to left) in the lead.

31 May 1918
Finally, the 2d Division heads east toward Château-Thierry. However, the deployment muddle leads to the haphazard, unorganized deployment of the division's units. Kitchens and division supply are strung out down the road to Meaux. One column includes the 5th Regiment, followed by the 23d Infantry, and the 3d Engineers marching to Montreuil, while the 6th Regiment is left far to the rear and the 6th Machine Gun Battalion experiences delays. The German *197th Division* moves up to take the right flank of the *Corps Conta* as it advances with the *237th Division* behind it.

1 June 1918
In the scrambled deployment, 2d Division troops arrive in no particular order and initially occupy a defensive line west of Château-Thierry. The 4th Brigade is assigned the sector to the left of the Paris-Metz road facing Belleau Wood (map 2). Marines assume defensive positions centered on the village of Lucy-le-Bocage. The brigade sector is bound by the village of Marigny-en-Orxois on the left and Triangle Farm on the right.

2 June 1918
German forces disposition at Belleau Wood is as follows (right to left): *197th Division, 237th Division,* and *10th Division.* The vanguard of the German right flank, the *197th Division,* advances to cross Clignon Brook and occupies the vicinity near the village of Belleau, north of the wood, as French forces withdraw through the Marines. At Les Mares Farm, outside of Marigny-en-Orxois, members of 2d Battal-

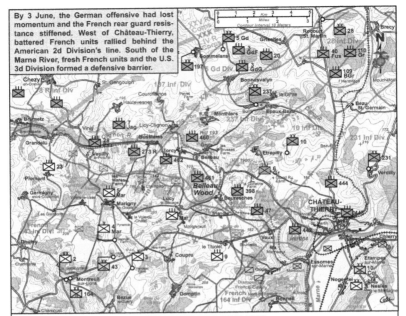

By 3 June, the German offensive had lost momentum and the French rear guard resistance stiffened. West of Château-Thierry, battered French units rallied behind the American 2d Division's line. South of the Marne River, fresh French units and the U.S. 3d Division formed a defensive barrier.

SITUATION ON 3 JUNE 1918

Initially, the U.S. 2d Division units were attached to the French 43d and 164th Divisions. Taking position as they arrived on the field and thinly spread on a front of 15 km, soldiers of the 3d Brigade were split on both flanks, with Marines of the 4th Brigade in the center. This shows the deployment of forces on 3 June as the last exhausted rear guard French elements withdrew and regrouped behind the line formed by the Marines and soldiers of the 2d Division. During the evening of 3 June, the Marines of 2d Battalion, 5th Regiment, repulsed the attack of the German *273d Reserve Infantry Regiment, 197th Division*, at Les Mares Farm; this would be as close as the German Army would get to Paris for the remainder of the war. During 4–5 June, both sides regrouped. The 2d Division took command of its sector and reorganized with the 4th Brigade on the left and 3d Infantry Brigade on the right. The division's front was reduced to 8 km and fresh French divisions moved into line on the flanks. The stage was set for the Allies to counterattack and steal the momentum from the enemy.

Map 2. Disposition of the brigade, June 1918.
Map by LtCol R. L. "Bill" Cody, USMC (Ret)

ion, 5th Regiment, dig in and show the Germans the effects of long-distance marksmanship. German artillery fire and infantry raids harass the Marines as they settle in along the brigade's front line.

3 June 1918

The fight for Les Mares Farm begins in earnest with German artillery preparation in the morning followed by infantry assaults by the *2d Battalion, 273d Regiment, 197th Division,*

Figure 5. Marines digging in near Lucy-le-Bocage, 1 June 1918.
The Print Collector, Alamy stock photo

reinforced by the *26th Reserve Jaeger Battalion* in the afternoon (figure 5). When advised to withdraw by a French
officer, Captain Lloyd W. Williams, 51st Company commander, replies, "Retreat, Hell! We just got here!"[7] Then-
First Lieutenant Lemuel C. Shepherd Jr. distinguishes
himself as a platoon leader in the 55th Company, manning
a forward outpost a few hundred yards beyond the farm.[8]
Shepherd and his Marines abandon their vantage point as
the assaulting Germans and heavy artillery fire threaten to
engulf them.

Accurate rifle fire from the Marines around the farm sty-
mies the assault that converges on the farm buildings. This
attack is considered the closest the Germans ever advance to-

[7] While attributed to Williams, the identity of the person who spoke these immor-
tal words is not exactly clear.
[8] Gen Shepherd (1896–1990) was 20th Commandant of the Marine Corps. He was
commissioned a second lieutenant on 11 April 1917 and joined the 5th Regiment,
which sailed to France that summer. For his gallantry in action at Belleau Wood,
including the defense of Les Mares Farm, Lt Shepherd was awarded the Army Distinguished Service Cross, the Navy Cross, the French Croix de Guerre, and was
cited in the general orders of the 2d Infantry Division, AEF.

DEFENSE OF LES MARES FARM
Evening of 3 June 1918

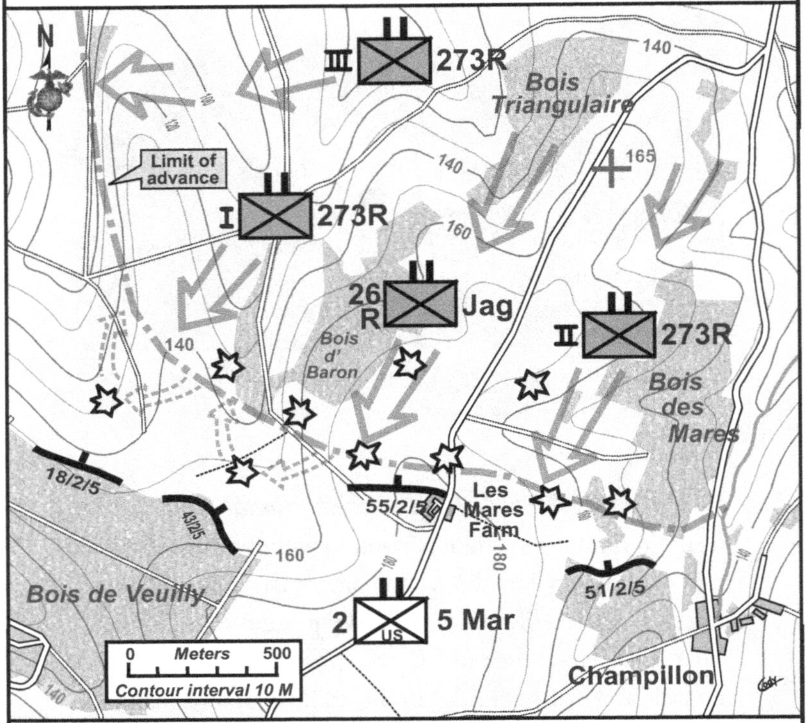

Accurate, long-range rifle fire by Marines of the 2d Battalion, 5th Regiment, supported by machine guns and artillery, stopped the massed attack of the German *197th Division's 273d Reserve Infantry Regiment*, reinforced with the *26th Reserve Jaeger Battalion*, in front of Les Mares Farm. This action, plus stiffened resistance all along the Allied line, stood as the high-water mark of the German spring offensive's Operation Blucher. In the fierce battles that followed, the Allies seized the initiative and kept it for the rest of the war.

Map 3. Allied defenses.
Map by LtCol R. L. "Bill" Cody, USMC (Ret)

ward the French capital. Halting the German advance at Les Mares Farm is remarkable when we consider the significant failure in coordination between 2d Battalion, 5th Regiment, around Les Mares Farm and 1st Battalion, 6th Regiment, on their right a kilometer north of Champillon (map 3). The

Figure 6. German machine gun team in the defense.
British Imperial War Museums

Germans attack directly at the farm, failing to take advantage of the gap between the two Marine battalions. Poor coordination between battalions from different regiments will be a recurring problem during the battle. The 2d Division's 2d Field Artillery Brigade finally arrives with the artillery regiments moving to their assembly areas near the front. The 12th Field Artillery Regiment is assigned to support the 4th Brigade and establishes its headquarters at La Loge Farm.

Following a French withdrawal about midnight on 2 June, by the evening of the 3d, soldiers of the German *461st Regiment, 237th Division*, occupy the entire forest of Belleau Wood and dig in (figure 6). The German regimental commander, Major Josef Bischoff, prepares extensive defensive positions in-depth.[9] As described later by then-Brigadier General James G. Harbord, the 4th Brigade commander, Belleau Wood is approximately 1.6 square kilometers with a dense tangle of undergrowth.

> *The topography of the greater part of the wood, especially in the eastern and southern portions, was extremely rugged and rocky, none of which was shown in any map available at the time. Great irregular boulders . . . were piled up and over and against one another. . . . These afforded shelter for machine-gun nests, with disposition in depth and flanking one another, generally so rugged that only direct hits of artillery were effective against them.*

In addition, the German *237th Division* is supported by the *83d Field Artillery Regiment*, which was organized for mobile operations with close combat groups supporting each infantry battalion. These units generally included light artillery guns, trench mortars, and light field howitzers designed to accompany infantry. The new light artillery guns were purpose-built lighter versions of the venerable 77mm field gun and designed to be pulled by horses with the artillerymen on foot (figure 7). This operational concept provided direct support in the offense to overcome machine gun nests and strong points and defeat counterattacks with the guns directly under control of battalion commanders.

---

[9] LtCol Josef Bischoff (1872–1948) was a much-decorated professional officer. Bischoff served in Africa during the German Colonial Wars in East and Southwest Africa for which he was twice decorated for valor. Prior to Belleau Wood, he served on the western front from 1914 to 1915, in the Sinai Campaign of 1916, and on the eastern front in 1917. His decorations for gallantry include the Iron Cross, first and second class; the Ottoman Gallipoli Star; and the Hohenzollern Knights Cross with Swords. The Knights Cross with Swords was an intermediate award between the Iron Cross first class and the Pour le Mérite for junior Prussian officers. Bischoff was awarded the Pour le Mérite on 30 June 1918 for his defense of Belleau Wood. This decoration was Imperial Germany's highest award for gallantry, or equivalent to the U.S. Medal of Honor.

Figure 7. German gunners manning a 7.7mm field artillery gun
in the Champagne region.
British Imperial War Museums

4 June 1918

German artillery fire and probing raids harass the Marines as
they dig in along the front line running generally from Les
Mares Farm on the left to Triangle Farm on the right. The
disposition of the Marine brigade is consolidated as follows:
5th Regiment on the left and 6th Regiment on the right with
Lucy-le-Bocage as the center. With the arrival of the rolling
kitchens the previous day, some Marines receive hot meals
for the first time since 31 May.

5 June 1918

Unknown to the Allies, the German offensive actually ran
out of steam, reaching its culminating point on 4 June due to
physical exhaustion and a lack of supplies. Both sides order
an operational pause to consolidate. The French XXI Corps
commander orders the 2d Division to recapture Belleau
Wood on 6 June, believing the Germans only hold a corner
of the wood. The main assault falls to the unit in that sector,
the 4th Brigade.

6 June 1918

The day results in catastrophe for the Marine Corps. Two assaults take place. The 1st Battalion, 5th Regiment, attempts to secure an area identified as Hill 142 on the brigade's left flank early in the morning; then 5th Regiment's 3d Battalion, and 3d Battalion, 6th Regiment, attack simultaneously late in the afternoon to seize Belleau Wood, the village of Bouresches, and an elevated railroad embankment at the northern edge of the village on the brigade's right (map 4). The assault on Belleau Wood, commanded by 6th Regiment's Colonel Albertus W. Catlin, comes in two phases: take Belleau Wood and then occupy Bouresches and the village railroad station. Major Thomas Holcomb's 2d Battalion, 6th Regiment, moves to support the right of the regiment's 3d Battalion as the battle progresses.

Late in the evening of 5 June, orders are issued to the 1st Battalion, 5th Regiment, for an attack at 0345 the next day. However, elements of the battalion are in several different locations and the battalion receives the command to attack a short time before the actual H-hour. Thus, the battalion staff scrambles to get their forces to the line of departure. Remarkably, the battalion attacks as directed at 0345 but with only two companies. Despite the lack of preparation, the first Marine Corps offensive of the war begins well as the attack hits the seam between two German divisions: the *197th* and the *237th*. The German units at the boundary apparently have some disagreement over which unit is responsible for this area. The American 49th Company on the right, commanded by Captain George W. Hamilton (1892–1922), inadvertently assaults beyond the objective, approaching Torcy. As Hamilton's Marines fight their way back to the objective, they fall on the rear of the German positions. Thus, the Marines penetrate between enemy units, attacking from the flanks and from the rear almost simultaneously.

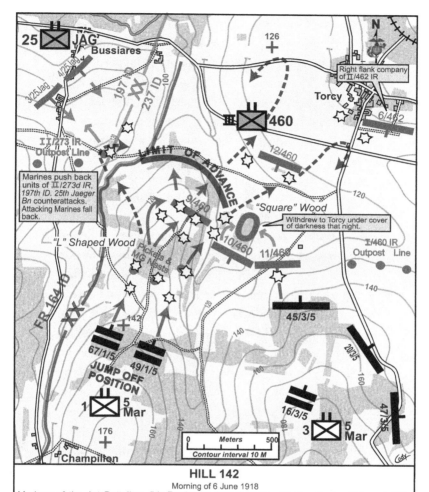

HILL 142

Morning of 6 June 1918

Marines of the 1st Battalion, 5th Regiment, launched the attack with the 49th and 67th Companies (17th and 66th Companies joined the fight later). The 67th Company overran the German *9th Company, 460th Infantry Regiment*, while the 49th Company brushed past the *10th Company*. Later, the 45th Company, 3d Battalion, 5th Regiment, on the right flank engaged the German *11th Company, 460th Infantry Regiment*, which formed a defensive perimeter with the *10th Company*. Many attacking Marines surged past the objective but withdrew to the limit of advance. The Marines held against several German counterattacks.

Map 4. The fight for Hill 142.
Map by LtCol R. L. "Bill" Cody, USMC (Ret)

However, on the 1st Battalion's left flank, First Lieutenant Orlando C. Crowther's 67th Company advances across open terrain and is decimated by flanking fire from its left as the German *25th Jaeger Battalion* counterattacks. Even with these losses, the attack succeeds with the timely arrival of other elements of the battalion and supporting machine guns. The reinforcements also include soldiers from 2d Division's 2d Engineer Regiment who, although only intended to help the Marines dig in, fight as riflemen, a continuing theme throughout the battle. Casualties, however, are heavy.[10]

At 1700, the second attack begins but fails against Major Bischoff's well-placed forces in Belleau Wood. Poor coordination between the assault battalions from different regiments, lack of artillery preparation due to concerns about surprise, and inadequate intelligence contributes to this failure as the German defenders are prepared and able to shift support to threatened areas. Coordination between attacking units suffers when Colonel Albertus W. Catlin, commanding the 6th Regiment and the entire attack, is severely wounded while observing the battle near Lucy-le-Bocage.[11] With his evacuation, Lieutenant Colonel Harry Lee, the 6th Regiment's executive officer, some distance in the rear, assumes command of the assault and what coordination there is suffers as a consequence.

The attack against the woods proper is grim as 3d Battalion, 5th Regiment, crosses a wheat field where the Marines are exposed to machine gun fire from concealed positions in the woods (map 5). While on the right, the 3d Battalion, 6th Regiment, fares better being closer to the woods at the beginning. Stragglers from 5th Regiment filter back to the line of departure, leaving the field littered with dead and dying Ma-

---

[10] Crowther is later awarded a Distinguished Service Cross (posthumously). GySgt Ernest A. Janson, 49th Company, who enlisted as Charles F. Hoffman (having previously deserted from the Army), is awarded the Medal of Honor for effectively stopping a German counterattack as the battalion consolidated its positions.

[11] Col Catlin (1868–1933) was awarded the Medal of Honor for gallantry at Vera Cruz in 1914.

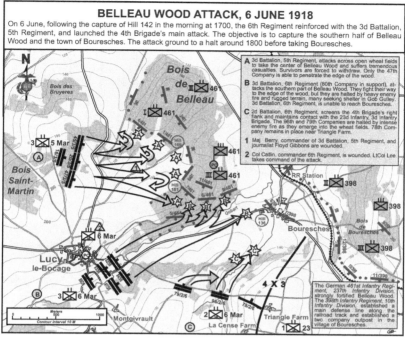

BELLEAU WOOD ATTACK, 6 JUNE 1918

On 6 June, following the capture of Hill 142 in the morning at 1700, the 6th Regiment reinforced with the 3d Battalion, 5th Regiment, and launched the 4th Brigade's main attack. The objective is to capture the southern half of Belleau Wood and the town of Bouresches. The attack ground to a halt around 1800 before taking Bouresches.

A 3d Battalion, 5th Regiment, attacks across open wheat fields to take the center of Belleau Wood and suffers tremendous casualties. Survivors are forced to withdraw. Only the 47th Company is able to penetrate the edge of the wood.

B 3d Battalion, 6th Regiment (80th Company in support), attacks the southern part of Belleau Wood. They fight their way to the edge of the wood, but they are halted by heavy enemy fire and rugged terrain, many seeking shelter in Gob Gulley. 3d Battalion, 6th Regiment, is unable to reach Bouresches.

C 2d Battalion, 6th Regiment, screens the 4th Brigade's right flank and maintains contact with the 23d Infantry, 3d Infantry Brigade. The 96th and 79th Companies are halted by intense enemy fire as they emerge into the wheat fields. 78th Company remains in place near Triangle Farm.

1 Maj Berry, commander of 3d Battalion, 5th Regiment, and journalist Floyd Gibbons are wounded.

2 Col Catlin, commander 6th Regiment, is wounded. LtCol Lee takes command of the attack.

The German 461st Infantry Regiment, 237th Infantry Division, strongly fortified Belleau Wood. The 398th Infantry Regiment, 10th Infantry Division, established a main defense line along the railroad track and established a two company outpost in the village of Bouresches.

Map 5. Marines attack the woods.
Map by LtCol R. L. "Bill" Cody, USMC (Ret)

rines and Navy corpsmen. Other survivors on the right flank of the attack join those from the 6th Regiment in the shelter of the woods. Newspaper correspondent Floyd Gibbons accompanies the attacking men and is severely wounded.[12] Later, his account publishes the infamous words supposedly shouted by Gunnery Sergeant Daniel J. Daly at the beginning of the attack: "Come on, you sons of bitches, do you

---

[12] Gibbons (1887–1939) was a well-known newspaper correspondent. In his wartime memoir *And They Thought We Wouldn't Fight* (1918), he claimed he heard "an old gunnery sergeant" exhort men to advance on 6 June, though it could never be corroborated.

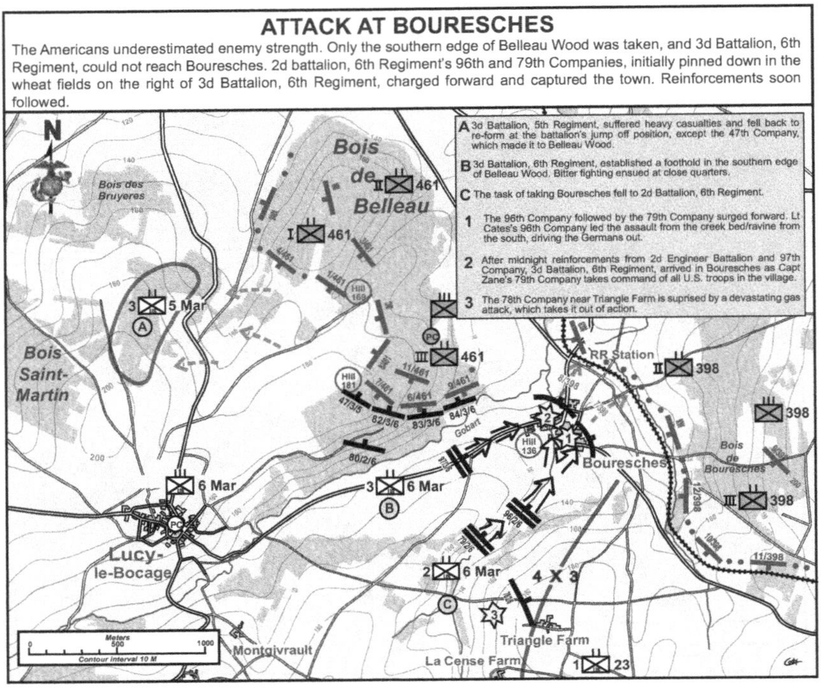
ATTACK AT BOURESCHES
The Americans underestimated enemy strength. Only the southern edge of Belleau Wood was taken, and 3d Battalion, 6th Regiment, could not reach Bouresches. 2d battalion, 6th Regiment's 96th and 79th Companies, initially pinned down in the wheat fields on the right of 3d Battalion, 6th Regiment, charged forward and captured the town. Reinforcements soon followed.
A 3d Battalion, 5th Regiment, suffered heavy casualties and fell back to re-form at the battalion's jump off position, except the 47th Company, which made it to Belleau Wood.
B 3d Battalion, 6th Regiment, established a foothold in the southern edge of Belleau Wood. Bitter fighting ensued at close quarters.
C The task of taking Bouresches fell to 2d Battalion, 6th Regiment.
1 The 96th Company followed by the 79th Company surged forward. Lt Cates's 96th Company led the assault from the creek bed/ravine from the south, driving the Germans out.
2 After midnight reinforcements from 2d Engineer Battalion and 97th Company, 3d Battalion, 6th Regiment, arrived in Bouresches as Capt Zane's 79th Company takes command of all U.S. troops in the village.
3 The 78th Company near Triangle Farm is suprised by a devastating gas attack, which takes it out of action.
N
Bois des Bruyeres
Bois de Belleau
Bois Saint-Martin
Lucy-le-Bocage
Bouresches
RR Station
Bois de Bouresches
Triangle Farm
La Cense Farm
Montgivrault
Hill 169
Hill 181
Hill 136
5 Mar
6 Mar
461
398
23
Gobart
4 X 3
Meters
0 500 1000
Contour interval 10 M

Map 6. Marines organize their defenses.
Map by LtCol R. L. "Bill" Cody, USMC (Ret)

want to live forever?"[13] Regrettably, the overall attack seizes only a small corner of the wood in the southwest (map 6).

Fortunately, the village of Bouresches is captured by elements of 2d Battalion, 6th Regiment, after the advance of the regiment's 3d Battalion reaches a stalemate. Casualties in the 2d Battalion are heavy as the Marines attack across the open fields north of Triangle Farm. Members of the battalion's 96th Company use a sheltered ravine to avoid enemy fire and infiltrate into the village directly from the

[13] SgtMaj Daniel Daly (1873–1937) was once acclaimed by MajGen John A. Lejeune, former Commandant of the Marine Corps, as "the outstanding Marine of all time." He received the nation's highest military award—the Medal of Honor—twice for separate acts of heroism.

south. Another future Commandant of the Marine Corps, then-Second Lieutenant Clifton B. Cates, enters the village, organizes the defense, and finds First Lieutenant James Robertson, now commanding the 96th Company, continuing the attack with a handful of Marines. Remarkably, Robertson leaves Cates in charge and returns to the rear. Cates seizes the initiative and leads the remaining Marines as they expel the German defenders who were from the *398th Infantry Regiment*.[14]

The defense of the village proves difficult due to the fact that any attempt to reinforce it receives heavy German fire from the railroad embankment and German positions in Belleau Wood. Acts of personal bravery kept the Marines supplied via the road from Lucy-le-Bocage. Darkness enables reinforcements from the division's 2d Engineer Regiment and the 79th Company, 3d Battalion, 6th Regiment, to reinforce the village. Cates relinquishes command to Captain Randolph T. Zane, 79th Company commander.[15] At the end of the day, 1st Battalion, 5th Regiment, holds the position north of Hill 142, but the poorly coordinated attack on Belleau Wood leaves 3d Battalion, 5th Regiment, unable to

---

[14] Gen Cates (1893–1970), 19th Commandant of the Marine Corps, as a second lieutenant in the Reserve, he reported for active duty at the Marine Barracks Port Royal, SC, on 13 June 1917 and sailed for France the following January. He is one of the few officers of any Service who commanded a platoon, a company, a battalion, a regiment, and a division under fire, bringing him nearly 30 decorations. He was awarded the Navy Cross, the Army Distinguished Service Cross, and an oak leaf cluster in lieu of a second award for heroism at Bouresches and Belleau Wood, in which he was both gassed and wounded. He received the Silver Star Medal at Soissons, where he was wounded a second time, and an oak leaf cluster in lieu of a second award in the Blanc Mont fighting. Navy dentist Lt (JG) Weedon E. Osborne was awarded the Medal of Honor (posthumously) for attempting to save Capt Donald F. Duncan, 96th Company commander, during the assault on Bouresches. The railroad embankment outside the village proved a formidable obstacle and remained in German hands throughout the battle.

[15] Capt Zane (1887–1918) died on 24 October 1918 at Brest, France, of wounds received at Belleau Wood on 26 June 1918. He is buried at the Somme American Military Cemetery, Bony, France. He was awarded the Navy Cross and Distinguished Army Cross for his leadership during the defense of Bouresches.

continue and the 3d Battalion, 6th Regiment, struggles to maintain a toehold in the southwest edge. Casualties for the day include 1,087 Americans and 452 German officers and enlisted.

7 June 1918

Mostly a quiet day as U.S. forces prepare to renew the offensive and the German units bring in reinforcements. For the next week, the southern half of Belleau Wood and Bouresches remains the focal point of severe fighting.

8 June 1918

A renewed assault by 3d Battalion, 6th Regiment, fails to gain ground. The Marines withdraw to Gobert Ravine (or "Gob Gully" to the Marines) to permit U.S. artillery to attack the woods as German artillery retaliates and leaves many Marine casualties as a result. During the evening, 1st Battalion, 6th Regiment, relieves 3d Battalion, 6th Regiment. The Germans reorganize the defense of Belleau Wood with the *40th Fusilier Regiment, 28th Division*, replacing Major Bischoff's *461st Regiment*, in the southern portion. Still responsible for the remaining half of the woods, Major Bischoff raises strong concerns about the inadequate dispositions of the *40th Fusiliers'* units in the dense undergrowth. Bischoff counsels that the *40th Fusiliers* have placed too few men forward and the counterattacking forces are too far back.

9 June 1918

An order for a Marine brigade attack against the wood is issued for the next morning and the units move into position late in the evening.

10 June 1918

New planned attacks by the 1st Battalion, 6th Regiment,

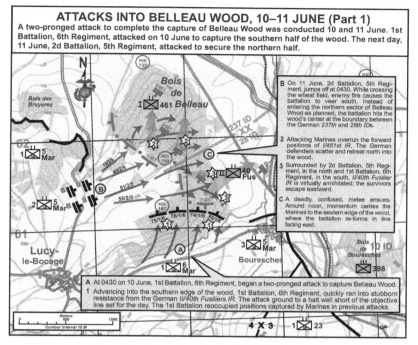

ATTACKS INTO BELLEAU WOOD, 10–11 JUNE (Part 1)

A two-pronged attack to complete the capture of Belleau Wood was conducted 10 and 11 June. 1st Battalion, 6th Regiment, attacked on 10 June to capture the southern half of the wood. The next day, 11 June, 2d Battalion, 5th Regiment, attacked to secure the northern half.

B On 11 June, 2d Battalion, 5th Regiment, jumps off at 0430. While crossing the wheat field, enemy fire causes the battalion to veer south. Instead of entering the northern sector of Belleau Wood as planned, the battalion hits the wood's center at the boundary between the German 237th and 28th IDs.

2 Attacking Marines overrun the forward positions of I/461st IR. The German defenders scatter and retreat north into the wood.

3 Surrounded by 2d Battalion, 5th Regiment, in the north and 1st Battalion, 6th Regiment, in the south, II/40th Fusilier IR is virtually annihilated; the survivors escape eastward.

C A deadly, confused, melee ensues. Around noon, momentum carries the Marines to the eastern edge of the wood, where the battalion re-forms in line facing east.

A At 0430 on 10 June, 1st Battalion, 6th Regiment, began a two-pronged attack to capture Belleau Wood.

1 Advancing into the southern edge of the wood, 1st Battalion, 6th Regiment, quickly ran into stubborn resistance from the German II/40th Fusiliers IR. The attack ground to a halt well short of the objective line set for the day. The 1st Battalion reoccupied positions captured by Marines in previous attacks.

Map 7. Marines on the offensive in Belleau Wood.
Map by LtCol R. L. "Bill" Cody, USMC (Ret)

directly into the southern edge of the wood begin at 0430, now supported by the 1st Battalion, 15th Field Artillery Regiment. Back to full strength with replacements, 3d Battalion, 5th Regiment, relieves 2d Battalion, 6th Regiment, in Bouresches (map 7). Again, Navy corpsmen are praised for their support of casualties.

11 June 1918

The 2d Battalion, 5th Regiment, attacks across the same open field as 3d Battalion, 5th Regiment, five days earlier, though still littered with bodies and abandoned equipment. With continued artillery support and pressure from 1st Battalion, 6th Regiment, the 2d Battalion, 5th Regiment, attacks and strikes the boundary between the *1st Battalion, 46ist Regiment*, and the *2d Battalion, 40th Fusiliers*. Although meeting stiff resistance, the assaulting companies on the right turn south to find 1st Battalion, 6th Regiment. Unfortunately for the Germans defenders, the Marines collide with the right flank of the *40th Fusiliers*. As noted in the *2d Battalion, 40th Fusiliers*'s War Diary, the Marines attack through the sector of the *46ist Regiment*, which meant they were already in the rear of the two forward German companies of the Fusiliers. Almost simultaneously, elements of 1st Battalion, 6th Regiment, attack the *40th Fusiliers* on the other flank. Thus, the forward units of the *2d Battalion, 40th Fusiliers*, are attacked in both flanks, decimating the battalion and driving survivors from the woods (maps 8 and 9). Colonel John W. Thomason Jr. describes the scene:

> *Under such pressure, the two companies of the* 40th *were torn to pieces, and their heavy machine gun defense broken up. The support and reserve companies, approaching from the east were caught in flanking fire from [the Marines in] Bouresches, and stopped. The developments anticipated by the* 461st Regiment *[Major Bischoff] . . . were all realized.*
>
> *A complete disaster was prevented by a counterattack from two companies of the* 461st Regiment, *but the Germans were not able to recover the territory lost. Now controlling the southern portion of the Belleau Wood, the Marines would direct their attention solely to the* 461st Regiment *to the north, the only German unit left in the woods. A German defeat was only a matter of time.*

However, confusion reigns on both sides due the dense undergrowth and terrain. Major Frederic Wise, commanding the 2d Battalion, 5th Regiment, and several subordinates become disoriented, and he erroneously reports he

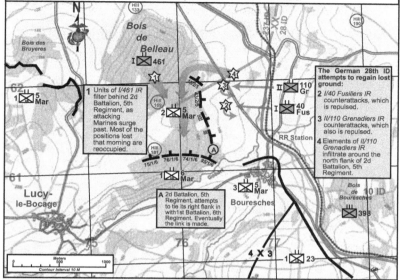

ATTACKS INTO BELLEAU WOOD, 10–11 JUNE (Part 2)

LtCol Wise, commander of 2d Battalion, 5th Regiment, around noon on 11 June realizes that during the confused, hand-to-hand fighting in the tangled woods that morning, the battalion had fought its way to the eastern edge of Belleau Wood not the northern. Under constant enemy pressure, preparations were made to change front under cover of darkness, then on the next day, make ready to continue the attack northward.

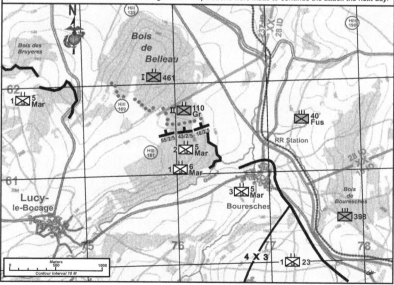

ATTACKS INTO BELLEAU WOOD, 10–11 JUNE (Part 3)

In the afternoon of 11 June, under constant enemy pressure, 2d Battalion, 5th Regiment, refused its left flank, pulled back, and by the end of the day had formed a line facing north with the 55th, 43d, and 18th Companies; 51st Company had suffered extremely heavy casualties and formed a small reserve. The 1st Battalion, 6th Regiment, took up support positions and tied in with the 2d Battalion's right flank. Preparations were made to continue the attack the next day.

Maps 8 and 9. Attack and counterattack in Belleau Wood.
Map by LtCol R. L. "Bill" Cody, USMC (Ret)

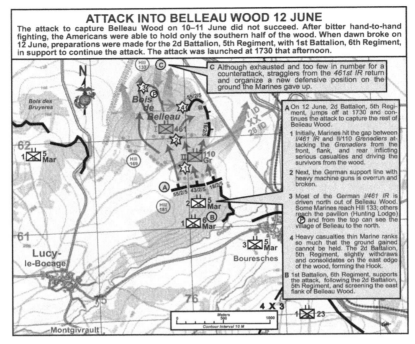

ATTACK INTO BELLEAU WOOD 12 JUNE

The attack to capture Belleau Wood on 10–11 June did not succeed. After bitter hand-to-hand fighting, the Americans were able to hold only the southern half of the wood. When dawn broke on 12 June, preparations were made for the 2d Battalion, 5th Regiment, with 1st Battalion, 6th Regiment, in support to continue the attack. The attack was launched at 1730 that afternoon.

C Although exhausted and too few in number for a counterattack, stragglers from the *461st IR* return and organize a new defensive position on the ground the Marines gave up.

A On 12 June, 2d Battalion, 5th Regiment, jumps off at 1730 and continues the attack to capture the rest of Belleau Wood.

1 Initially, Marines hit the gap between *I/461 IR* and *II/110 Grenadiers* attacking the *Grenadiers* from the front, flank, and rear inflicting serious casualties and driving the survivors from the wood.

2 Next, the German support line with heavy machine guns is overrun and broken.

3 Most of the German *I/461 IR* is driven north out of Belleau Wood. Some Marines reach Hill 133; others reach the pavilion (Hunting Lodge) and from the top can see the village of Belleau to the north.

4 Heavy casualties thin Marine ranks so much that the ground gained cannot be held. The 2d Battalion, 5th Regiment, slightly withdraws and consolidates on the east edge of the wood, forming the Hook.

B 1st Battalion, 6th Regiment, supports the attack, following the 2d Battalion, 5th Regiment, and screening the east flank of Belleau Wood.

Map 10. Holding the southern edge of the wood.
Map by LtCol R. L. "Bill" Cody, USMC (Ret)

has reached the northern edge of Belleau Wood. In reality, he is in the middle looking west. As night falls, the battalion begins to slowly regain cohesion and prepares to attack northward the next day.

12 June 1918

Advances on the eastern edge of the southern portion of the wood are lost when a German counterattack by two battalions of the *461st Regiment* reestablishes a defensive line. Elements of the *109th Grenadier Regiment, 28th Division*, almost recaptures Bouresches but are repulsed (map 10). Brigadier General Harbord holds a council of war and concludes that the German hold on the northern one-third of the wood is tenuous. An attack at 1800 achieves a breakthrough in the northern half of the woods, but Marines are left exposed. Due to casualties and influenza, a coordinated German counterattack to drive the Marines from the northern portion is postponed until the next day.

13 June 1918
Marines plug the line in their exposed area. Counterattacks by units of the *110th Grenadier* and *40th Fusilier Regiments* drive the Marines back as the Germans regain some lost ground at the eastern edges of the wood's southern portion. The U.S. 23d Infantry, 3d Brigade, on the 4th Brigade's right, begins to extend its left flank, assuming responsibility for Bouresches and freeing up more Marines for the conflict in the woods (map 11). A planned relief of 2d Battalion, 5th Regiment, is for naught as deploying Marines from the 2d Battalion, 6th Regiment, are caught in the dark by an artillery barrage with gas just prior to midnight.[16]

14 June 1918
Due to casualties from the German artillery, the relief of 2d Battalion, 5th Regiment, is postponed and 2d Battalion, 6th Regiment, survivors make their way into the woods and reinforce the 5th Regiment (map 12). Major Frederic Wise, commander of 2d Battalion, 5th Regiment, reports at 0605 that almost two companies of the 2d Battalion, 6th Regiment, have reported to him, noting that the "other two companies [are] badly broken up, from shells and gas." Another German counterattack fails with heavy losses. With that result and the outbreak of influenza on 9 June, the German higher headquarters abandons all operations to retake Belleau Wood. As noted in the German military's official history

---

[16] GySgt Fred W. Stockham was later awarded the Medal of Honor (posthumously) for saving one of his Marines when Stockham gave him his gas mask and carried him to the aid station near Lucy-le-Bocage. Stockham died several days later from the effects of the gas.

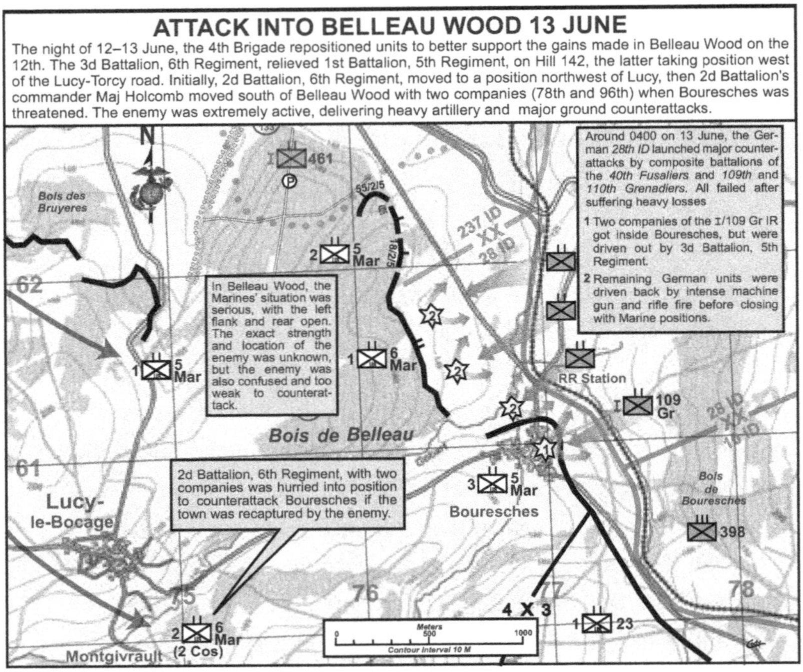

ATTACK INTO BELLEAU WOOD 13 JUNE

The night of 12–13 June, the 4th Brigade repositioned units to better support the gains made in Belleau Wood on the 12th. The 3d Battalion, 6th Regiment, relieved 1st Battalion, 5th Regiment, on Hill 142, the latter taking position west of the Lucy-Torcy road. Initially, 2d Battalion, 6th Regiment, moved to a position northwest of Lucy, then 2d Battalion's commander Maj Holcomb moved south of Belleau Wood with two companies (78th and 96th) when Bouresches was threatened. The enemy was extremely active, delivering heavy artillery and major ground counterattacks.

Map 11. Bouresches recaptured.
Map by LtCol R. L. "Bill" Cody, USMC (Ret)

of the war when discussing the fighting at Belleau Wood: "The fresh American troops proved to be quite worthy opponents."

15 June 1918

Heavy bombardment by the Germans continues as the Marines persist in the attack north but are stopped by the defenders. Relief of the 4th Brigade in Belleau Wood by the U.S. Army's 7th Infantry, 3d Division, begins (map 13). Allowing the Marines to recover from exhaustion and heavy casualties, 1st Battalion, 7th Infantry, relieves the 2d Battalion, 5th Regiment, and the 2d Battalion, 6th Regiment.

Having lost much of its combat effectiveness as well, the

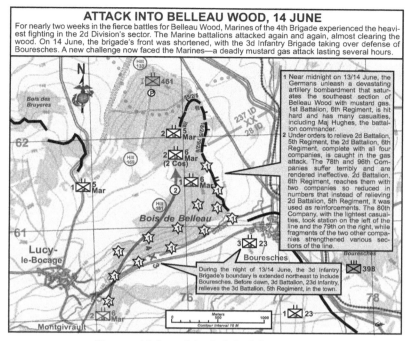

ATTACK INTO BELLEAU WOOD, 14 JUNE

For nearly two weeks in the fierce battles for Belleau Wood, Marines of the 4th Brigade experienced the heaviest fighting in the 2d Division's sector. The Marine battalions attacked again and again, almost clearing the wood. On 14 June, the brigade's front was shortened, with the 3d Infantry Brigade taking over defense of Bouresches. A new challenge now faced the Marines—a deadly mustard gas attack lasting several hours.

1 Near midnight on 13/14 June, the Germans unleash a devastating artillery bombardment that saturates the southeast section of Belleau Wood with mustard gas. 1st Battalion, 6th Regiment, is hit hard and has many casualties, including Maj Hughes, the battalion commander.

2 Under orders to relieve 2d Battalion, 5th Regiment, the 2d Battalion, 6th Regiment, complete with all four companies, is caught in the gas attack. The 78th and 96th Companies suffer terribly and are rendered ineffective. 2d Battalion, 6th Regiment, reaches them with two companies so reduced in numbers that instead of relieving 2d Battalion, 5th Regiment, it was used as reinforcements. The 80th Company, with the lightest casualties, took station on the left of the line and the 79th on the right, while fragments of the two other companies strengthened various sections of the line.

During the night of 13/14 June, the 3d Infantry Brigade's boundary is extended northeast to include Bouresches. Before dawn, 3d Battalion, 23d Infantry, relieves the 3d Battalion, 5th Regiment, in the town.

Map 12. 3d Infantry Brigade defends Bouresches.
Map by LtCol R. L. "Bill" Cody, USMC (Ret)

German *1st Battalion, 461st Regiment*, begins its withdrawal, replaced by the *3d Battalion, 347th Regiment, 87th Division*. As the Germans are pushed into the northern portion of the wood, the battlespace shrinks accordingly and, in effect, concentrates their combat power.

16 June 1918
Generally a quiet day as the 2d Battalion, 7th Infantry, relieves the 1st Battalion, 6th Regiment. The 3d Battalion, 6th Regiment, currently defending Hill 142, is relieved by a unit from the French 167th Division and becomes the division reserve.

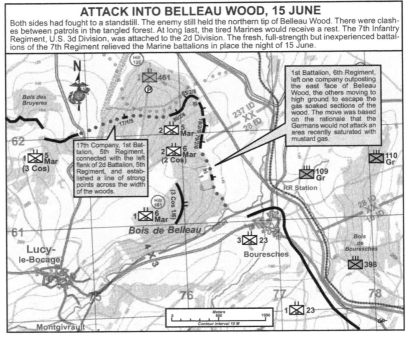

ATTACK INTO BELLEAU WOOD, 15 JUNE
Both sides had fought to a standstill. The enemy still held the northern tip of Belleau Wood. There were clashes between patrols in the tangled forest. At long last, the tired Marines would receive a rest. The 7th Infantry Regiment, U.S. 3d Division, was attached to the 2d Division. The fresh, full-strength but inexperienced battalions of the 7th Regiment relieved the Marine battalions in place the night of 15 June.

Map 13. Relief of 3d Division.
Map by LtCol R. L. "Bill" Cody, USMC (Ret)

17 June 1918

Relief of the Marine brigade by the 7th Infantry is complete. Three battalions of the 7th Infantry deploy into the woods under the command of the sector commander, Marine Colonel Wendell C. Neville, 5th Regiment, while Lieutenant Colonel Logan Feland, executive officer, 5th Regiment, commands inside the wood.[17] The 1st Battal-

---

[17] MajGen Wendell C. Neville (1870–1930), 14th Commandant of the Marine Corps, was commissioned a second lieutenant in 1892. He was awarded the Medal of Honor while in command of Marines landing at Vera Cruz, Mexico, on 21 April 1914. On 1 January 1918, he was placed in command of the 5th Regiment in France, and in May, he moved his regiment into action near Belleau Wood. In July 1918, Neville was promoted to brigadier general and given command of the entire 4th Brigade, which he directed during the remaining days of the war and during its occupation service in Germany.

ion, 7th Infantry, replaces the 2d Battalion, 5th Regiment.

18 June 1918
The day is reported as "quiet" by 4th Brigade. That night, the 1st Battalion, 7th Infantry, is repulsed with casualties when it attempts to straighten its lines and a company from the 3d Battalion successfully occupies former German positions on the Lucy-Torcy road that were not reoccupied during the German relief.

19 June 1918
Light action is reported by two 7th Infantry battalions as plans are drawn up for future attacks.

20 June 1918
The 1st and 3d Battalions, 7th Infantry, attack to dislodge the Germans from the woods. The 1st Battalion is stalled while the 3d Battalion makes limited unopposed gains. The German *237th* and *87th Divisions* complete reorganization in the northern edge of the woods.

21 June 1918
French Army III Corps assumes control of the sector. The last battalion-scale attack by Army units fails, leaving the northern portion of the woods still in German hands. The 7th Infantry soldiers are hit with heavy small-arms and artillery fire. The 1st Battalion suffers 170 casualties.

22 June 1918
Marine units replace the 7th Infantry on the front line. During the evening of 22–23 June, the 3d Battalion, 6th Regiment, replaces 1st Battalion, 7th Infantry, in the southern end of the wood. The 7th Infantry suffers 349 casualties (51 killed in action, 265 wounded in action, and 34 missing)

while providing the Marines time to rest and recover. French commanders reiterate demands that the entire woods be seized.

Germans begin final unit rotations with battalions of the *347th Regiment*. Taking advantage of the lull in the fighting, the Germans replace the *3d battalion, 347th Regiment*, with the regiment's *1st Battalion*. Major Maurice E. Shearer, now commanding the 3d Battalion, 5th Regiment, moves into the northern portion of the wood and plans for the final assault.

23 June 1918

With many replacements, 3d Battalion, 5th Regiment, returns to the fight and begins the final assault at 1900 with no gains and heavy losses against a stubborn defense by *1st Battalion, 347th Regiment, 87th Division*. Major Shearer advises that infantry alone will not push the Germans from the woods (map 14). At approximately the same time, 2d Battalion, 5th Regiment, replaces the 3d Battalion, 7th Infantry, in support of Shearer's battalion.

24 June 1918

The French command commits sufficient artillery to reduce the threat at the northern edge of the woods, agreeing to a divisional artillery attack. Marines prepare to withdraw back to the south of the center of the woods to avoid the approaching storm of steel.

25 June 1918

A major 14-hour bombardment starts at 0300 and makes clearance of the remaining woods possible. The following Marine attack overwhelms the remaining enemy machine gun outposts; the Marines and soldiers take many prisoners and inflict significant casualties on the *347th Regiment*. Marines and Army machine gunners participate in the as-

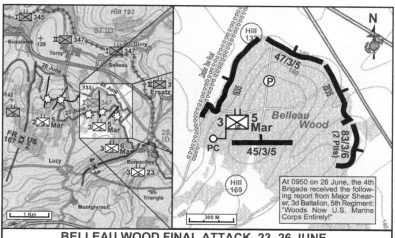

BELLEAU WOOD FINAL ATTACK, 23–26 JUNE

After a weeklong break, the Marine brigade goes back into action. During the night of 22–23 June, the Marines relieve the inexperienced soldiers of the 7th Infantry, who fought hard but made no gains against the Germans in Belleau Wood. In the meantime, the German *87th ID* had replaced the *237th ID*. *I Bn, 347th IR* of the former was assigned the defense of the north end of the wood. The 3d Battalion, 5th Regiment, moves into the front line facing the German *I/347 IR* and attacks on 23 June. Initially, the 3d Battalion makes headway but is forced back by heavy fire. On 25 June, after an intense artillery barrage, they attack again. The 3d Battalion, 6th Regiment, is in support, screening the east edge of the wood. The 2d Battalion, 5th Regiment, advances on the left of 3d Battalion, 5th Regiment, driving back the German outpost line. This time, they break through the left of the defending *I/347 IR*. The Germans fall back to positions near the village of Belleau. When dawn breaks on 26 June, the last German defenders have been driven from Belleau Wood, never to return.

Map 14. Germans driven from the wood.
Map by LtCol R. L. "Bill" Cody, USMC (Ret)

sault. Germans are finally forced to withdraw from Belleau Wood to defensive positions prepared along the Torcy-Belleau road.

26 June 1918

At 1000, the 4th Brigade's commanding general submits to the commanding general of 2d Division a supplement to his 25 June report on the action ending at 2000 on 25 June. This supplementary report notes that "all companies of Major Shearer's Third Battalion, Fifth Marines, now in position around the edge of BOIS DE BELLEAU. Major Shearer reports 'Woods now U.S. Marine Corps entirely'."

SUMMARY

The 4th Brigade began the assault against the Bois de Belleau on 6 June 1918. By the morning of 26 June, the battle was over and the woods had been cleared of Germans. The last unit of the 2d Division withdrew from the front on the night of 8–9 July. From then on, the honors poured in for the 4th Brigade and the division. Local French officials sent congratulatory messages to headquarters for stopping the German offensive, and press reports heralded the American victory. However, at what cost did this come to pass? Casualty numbers are difficult to assess for a variety of reasons. Author George B. Clark cites divisional orders when he reports the battle deaths for the brigade from 2 June to 5 July 1918 as 1,062, plus 33 missing. In addition, he highlights the 3,170 officers and men who were wounded in varying degrees, including 445 gas casualties.

Robert B. Asprey in his classic *At Belleau Wood* confirms that the price of glory was high: "From June 1 to July 10 the 2nd U.S. Division counted 217 officer and 9,560 enlisted casualties. Of these . . . the 4th Marine Brigade [lost] 126 officers and 5,057 men." Edward M. Coffman writes that there were approximately 5,200 casualties with 750 killed, accounting for more than 50 percent of the brigade's strength. An unofficial brigade history reports 665 killed in action and 3,633 wounded during the period of 1 June–16 July. In his 1928 Naval Institute's *Proceedings* article, retired German Army Lieutenant Colonel Ernst Otto notes German casualties were equally sanguinary: 881 killed in action and 2,637 wounded in action.

There are a number of reasons for such casualties in the fighting that took place in and around Belleau Wood, a crescent-shaped area approximately 1.6 kilometers long, running north to south. The Marines were fresh and untested. They exhibited what was described by German intelligence as a "careless confidence." A German private wrote home that they were "terribly reckless fellows." While such qualities can be admired, when exhibited in situations exacerbated by poor maps, inadequate communications, confusion at the front, inexperienced leaders, and a determined enemy defending heavily forested terrain, they can be the cause of much carnage.

What the Allies did know after 26 June 1918 was that the Americans had come to fight and the future of civilized society seemed more secure. At the conclusion of his 1928 article, Lieutenant Colonel Otto proposed that there be a monument erected on the edge of the scarred, blood-soaked wood. The inscription should read:

> *These are the woods of Belleau; in June, 1918, wrested from the French, after a brave defense, by the Germans, storming on in a bold two-day offensive; heroically defended by them for nine days; then taken by storm in two days, with incomparable bravery, by the Americans,*

who remained victoriously in possession of the woods.
Honor to the unexcelled heroes of the three nations who,
true to their Fatherland, here fought and died.

That is quite an epitaph.

THE OPPOSING FORCES

The 4th Brigade

In November 1918, the table of organization for a brigade headquarters showed 25 men (table 1).[18] Each regiment contained approximately 3,400 men, with the three infantry battalions totaling 1,027 each. An infantry company came to approximately 256 men. The machine gun company with each regiment was manned by 178 men, and the brigade's machine gun battalion numbered generally 759.

German Forces

In early June 1918, the 2d Division faced elements of the following German Army units in the 4th Brigade sector (from left to right): *197th Division*, *237th Division*, and *10th Division*. During the evening of 8–9 June 1918, the *28th Division* replaced the *10th Division* following its losses near

---

[18] These statistics were reported in *Order of Battle of the United States Land Forces in the World War: Organization of the American Expeditionary Forces, United States Army in the World War, 1917–1919*, vol. 1 (Washington, DC: Center of Military History, United States Army, 1988), 335–88.

Table 1. 4th Brigade table of organization

5th Regiment		
1st Battalion	2d Battalion	3d Battalion
17th (A) Company	18th (E) Company	16th (I) Company
49th (B) Company	43d (F) Company	20th (K) Company
66th (C) Company	51st (G) Company	45th (L) Company
67th (D) Company	55th (H) Company	47th (M) Company

8th Machine Gun Company
Supply Company
Headquarters Company

6th Regiment		
1st Battalion	2d Battalion	3d Battalion
74th (A) Company	78th (E) Company	82d (I) Company
75th (B) Company	79th (F) Company	83d (K) Company
76th (C) Company	80th (G) Company	84th (L) Company
95th (D) Company	96th (H) Company	97th (M) Company

73d Machine Gun Company
Supply Company
Headquarters Company

6th Machine Gun Battalion	
15th (A) Company	77th (C) Company
23d (B) Company	81st (D) Company

Bouresches, and the *5th Guards Division* took the place of the *197th Division* west of Belleau Wood. The *87th Division* relieved the survivors of the *237th* and *28th Divisions* in Belleau Wood area on 22 June, when they were withdrawn due to casualties.

The strength of a German division with its three regiments in 1918 was approximately 17,600, which was much smaller than an American division of about 27,000.[19] The basic infantry unit included the regiment of three battalions with four companies of infantry and one machine gun company with each battalion. By June

[19] *Histories of Two Hundred and Fifty-One Divisions of the German Army which Participated in the War (1914–1918)*, War Department Document No. 905 (Washington, DC: Government Printing Office, 1920). Reprinted by London Stamp Exchange, 1989, iv; and Robert B. Asprey, *At Belleau Wood* (New York: G. P. Putnam's Sons, 1965), 31.

1918, infantry battalions numbered about 718 soldiers.[20]

The *5th Guards Division* was organized in February 1917; it participated in the Aisne offensive during 27–30 May 1918, and then between 31 May and 7 June, it was in reserve. It was heavily engaged near Torcy after 7 June against the Marines' 4th Brigade, resulting in considerable casualties. Several companies of the *20th Regiment* were destroyed on 8–9 June, while others were reduced to 30–40 men. The division lost about one-half of its effective strength in this period. It was withdrawn from the line on 30 June and reconstituted in reserve of the Torcy sector during 1–17 July. The *5th Guards Division* was rated a first-class division; but after heavy fighting near Torcy, its value as an attack division had been significantly reduced.[21]

The German *197th Division* was created in August 1916 on the eastern front and made its first appearance on the western front in March 1918, holding the quiet Chemin des Dames sector until the Aisne offensive began on 27 May. Attack divisions passed through the *197th Division*, which followed up in close reserve, and was engaged on 31 May northwest of Château-Thierry. The *273d Regiment* experienced heavy fighting while opposite French forces and the U.S. 2d Division at Les Mares Farm and Hill 142 before be-

---

[20] David T. Zabecki, *The German 1918 Offensives: A Case Study in the Operational Level of War* (London, New York: Routledge, 2006), 89.

[21] Initially, the AEF graded the quality of the German divisions in 1918 using the French-produced evaluations/histories as an initial basis because the French Army had estimated the value of each German division in earlier years. For the Americans, the evaluation was done by the G-2 (intelligence), General Headquarters, AEF. The quality or class was a changing grade or estimate based on known abilities of the unit. As the war wore on, many of the divisions considered first class were downgraded as old men, young boys, and even the infirm were brought into some of the divisions. The G-2 used frontline U.S. reports and interviews to grade a unit according to four classes: first-class division, second-class division, third-class division, and fourth-class division. At the beginning of the war, certain units were rated first class; for example, infantry divisions were the best. Later, it was necessary to track the combat efficiency of the German divisions to gauge the caliber of the opposing force.

ing relieved on 8 June. The division was rated as third class. It suffered such heavy casualties and loss of morale in June 1918 that it was dissolved in October.

The *10th Division* was mobilized in 1914 in Posen, Prussia (now Poland). Prior to 1918, the division and its units had a good reputation, although it did not perform as well as expected at Verdun in 1917. For the Third Battle of the Aisne in 1918, the *10th Division* attacked along the Chemin des Dames on 27 May. It remained in front of the advance until reaching the vicinity of Bouresches around 30 May; however, by 4 June, the division had suffered heavily. Many companies of the *47th Infantry Regiment* were without officers. With its companies averaging about 40 men, the *398th Infantry Regiment* reported that it was no longer fit for frontline service. The *6th Grenadier Regiment* was exhausted and incapable of further effort. Needing approximately 2,700–3,000 replacements, the division was withdrawn from Bouresches between 8 and 10 June 1918 and replaced by the *28th Division*. The division was rated in 1918 as a first-class division. It performed very well in the 1918 offensives, but never recovered from the fighting in June and July.

The *28th Division* was organized at the beginning of the war; this division came from the Grand Duchy of Baden in the southwest on the east bank of the Rhine. It spent much of the war on the defensive in the west; but in February 1918, it began training for offensive operations. It fought in the Battle of the Somme in March and distinguished itself, though at a heavy cost. Some companies lost 75 percent of their manpower. In April, it received 2,500 reinforcements, with a large share being young 18-year-old conscripts. On 27 May 1918, the division was used as an attack division, covering 60 kilometers by 3 June, as it was considered a first-class unit. The division commander, Major General Hans Freiherr Prince von Buchau, was killed on 29 May. Out of the line during 3–8 June, it relieved the *10th Division* and reentered near Bouresches opposite the 4th Brigade until withdrawn on 3 July. It suffered heavy losses during the fighting in Belleau Wood on 10–11 June, especially the *2d Battalion, 40th Fusilier Regiment*. Following its fighting in Belleau Wood in June, the *28th Division* was not seriously engaged until it fought again in defense of the American's Meuse-Argonne offensive in the fall.

The *87th Division* was organized in June 1915 and was engaged from the beginning in the eastern front. During the 1918 spring offensive, it held a quiet sector until 18 June, when it was relieved and then entered the line on 22 June at Belleau Wood. During this period, the division was heavily engaged in hard fighting with the 4th Brigade. Driven from the woods on 25–26 June, the *347th Regiment* suffered heavily given the number that were killed and wounded in addition to 300 prisoners that were taken. Afterward, it took part in the German retreat until 26 July, when it was withdrawn from the front until the end of August. Upon its return to the war on 26 August 1918, the division again suffered heavy losses during fighting through the end of September. Although this division was one of the most heterogeneous in the Prussian Army, it was considered a fourth-class unit. It had received a large draft of young recruits from across Germany in November 1917. Arriving at the western front at the end of March 1918, it was assessed as having mediocre combat value.

The *197th Division* was created on the eastern front in August 1916, and it did not make an appearance on the western front until March 1918, holding the quiet Chemin des Dames sector until participating in the Aisne offensive on 27 May. Attack divisions passed through the *197th*, which followed up in close reserve, only to be engaged on 31 May northwest of Château-Thierry. The *273d Regiment* experienced heavy fighting while opposite French forces and the U.S. 2d Division at Les Mares Farm and Hill 142 before being relieved on 8 June. The *197th Division* was rated as third class, suffering such heavy casualties and loss of morale in June 1918 that it was dissolved in October.

The *237th Division* was organized in January 1917 primarily from young conscripts and returned sick and wounded from the front, principally from the Rhine District. In 1918, the division included the *244th Brigade (Infantry)* made up of the *460th Regiment*, *461st Regiment*, and the *462d Regiment*. In addition to cavalry, artillery, transport, and medical units, it also included the *237th Pioneer Battalion (Engineers)* and the *237th Signal Command*. Its artillery regiment was the *83d Field Artillery Regiment* with a *Sturmkanone Battery*. With its combat value considered mediocre in 1917 with service in Russia, it likely did not take part in the May 1918 offensive until it reached Belleau Wood on 1 June. The division suffered heavy casualties during the weeks of intense fighting and was withdrawn by 22 June. The division received 2,000 replacements before being withdrawn entirely from the front on 14 August. Returning to the front in September, it participated in the defensive battles until the end of the war. In October 1918, the division numbered approximately 800 men. The *237th Division* was rated a fourth-class division, although it was considered to have veteran leaders and excellent regimental commanders. The *460th Regiment* defended the eastern portion of Hill 142 while the *461st Regiment*, commanded by Major Josef Bischoff with Major Hans von Hartlieb, his best battalion commander, was responsible for defending Belleau Wood with the 3d Battalion for most of the month of June 1918.[22]

---

[22] LtCol Hans von Hartlieb genannt Walsporn (1871–1940).

BATTLEFIELD
ITINERARY AND
STANDS

CAUTION: the area covered by this field guide was a battlefield for almost a month. Unexploded ordnance has been found and continues to pose a threat to this day (figure 8). Relic hunting is illegal and can be hazardous to your health. In addition, many areas covered by the field guide are **private property** and should be treated accordingly. We are always guests. Leave nothing but footprints and take nothing but photographs.

Depending on the timing of your visit, the private farmland around Belleau Wood may contain growing crops. As this property belongs to working farms, you should use extreme care if walking through these fields during a growing season to avoid trampling any plants.

Introduction

Each stand has been selected for its relevance to the battle and ease of access via either privately owned vehicle or tour bus. The stands are noted on the accompanying map. Fur-

Figure 8. Unexploded ordnance in the woods.
Courtesy of SgtMaj Hubert Caloud, USMC (Ret)

ther, any walking at the stands will be kept to a minimum. However, several require some walking and proper footwear is recommended. The number of stands is limited so that the time devoted to the entire visit can be less than a full day. At each stand, the narrative will orient the reader to the terrain and the significance of the location (figure 9).

This tour begins with a stop at the Visitor Center, Aisne-Marne American Cemetery, Belleau, France, as the central focal point for the guide. You will return to the Visitor Center at the conclusion of the tour at Stand 8. The cemetery staff is very helpful and is available to answer questions about the area. Note that the times provided are approximations only as travel will vary according to traffic, weather, and other local factors. The tour averages about five hours but can be modified as your time and schedule permit. It is advisable to carry something to drink and eat.

Note: toilet facilities and places to eat in the area covered by this guide are scarce. The villages of Bouresches and

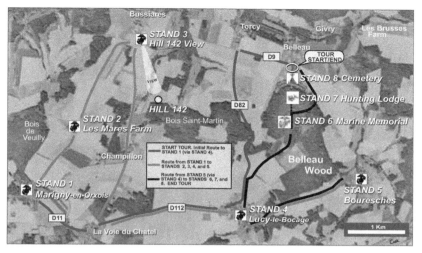

Figure 9. Itinerary overview.
Le Portail IGN, courtesy of LtCol R. L. "Bill" Cody, USMC (Ret)

Lucy-le-Bocage have local bars that may be open, but the availability of food is limited. The Visitor Center at the Aisne-Marne American Cemetery offers restrooms for visitors in the immediate vicinity. Plan accordingly for the safety and comfort of those in your group.

Directions to Stand 1 (Village of Marigny-en-Orxois) (travel duration: 15 minutes): proceed out the cemetery main gate and turn left (Route D9) in the direction of Bussiares. Pass the German Military Cemetery on your left. As a collecting point for casualties from the battles of World War I in the region, it contains the remains of 8,630 German soldiers. Turn left at the next intersection (Route D82) in the direction of Lucy-le-Bocage. Note that Belleau Wood is on your left as you head south. You will pass through a wooded area in which the Marines fought twice going from your right to left. Exiting the wooded area, you are now in the wheat field made famous by the 6 June attack. You will return to this area later. Once arriving in the center of Lucy-le-Bocage,

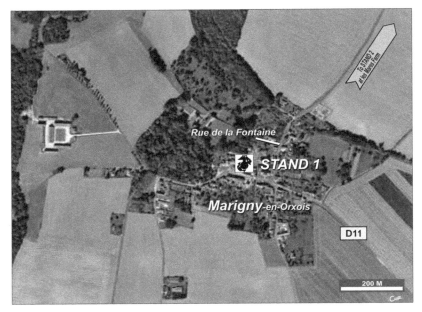

Figure 10. Stand 1 near Marigny-en-Orxois.
Le Portail IGN, courtesy of LtCol R. L. "Bill" Cody, USMC (Ret)

turn right on Route D112 toward La Voie du Châtel. Continue through La Voie du Châtel, bearing to the right toward Marigny-en-Orxois on Route D11. Proceed into the village and park in the village center near the picturesque medieval market hall (figure 10).

Stand 1. Village of Marigny-en-Orxois (travel duration: 15 minutes)

This village was basically the left flank of the 4th Brigade sector upon its deployment to the area. You will notice the medieval market hall in the village center (figure 11). It is one of the oldest such structures in France and is considered a national historical monument.

As the Marines arrived in the region, such places as Marigny-en-Orxois served as key assembly areas for the battalions prior to moving to their positions. These villages also

Figure 11. Marigny-en-Orxois market hall.
Courtesy of Gilles Lagin

Figure 12. Marines deploying to the front.
Marine Corps History Division

became locations for important support activities, such as supply and medical care. Surely, Marines from the 2d Battalion, 5th Regiment, assembled here in the village center as they prepared to move out to Les Mares Farm (figure 12). If you refer to the narrative for late May and early June (pp. 20–30), you can get an appreciation for the difficulty of the deployment.

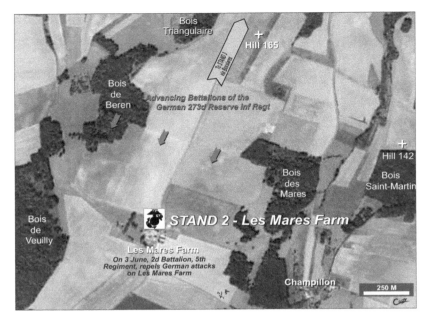

Figure 13. Stand 2 at Les Mares Farm.
Le Portail IGN, courtesy of LtCol R. L. "Bill" Cody, USMC (Ret)

Directions to Stand 2 (Les Mares Farm) (travel duration: 5 minutes): from the village center, drive back east on Route D11 and turn left (north) in the direction of Bussiares on Rue de la Fontaine. As you leave the village, you will note a cemetery on your right. The defilade area of the cemetery to the south was the headquarters of the 2d Battalion, 5th Regiment, during the fighting at Les Mares Farm. As you crest the ridge after the cemetery, you can see farm buildings in front of you. Proceed to the area of the farm and carefully pull over onto the shoulder at the northern edge of the farm (figure 13).

Stand 2. Les Mares Farm
(travel duration: 15 minutes)
The 2d Battalion, 5th Regiment, deployed to defend this

farm on 1 June 1918. German artillery fire and probing raids from the north harassed the Marines as they dug in along the front line. The battle raged in earnest by 4 June 1918, when the Germans from the *2d Battalion, 273d Regiment, 197th Division,* assaulted the Allies' positions at Les Mares Farm on the brigade's left flank. The current farm buildings represent the Marine main line of resistance occupied by a company. Two other companies were positioned to the west and one to the east. The 51st Company to the east was commanded by Captain Lloyd Williams, who legend has it gave the famous reply, "Retreat, Hell! We just got here!"[23] Regrettably, Williams did not survive the ensuing battle. If you look north, you can get a good appreciation of the ground over which the Germans attacked. Repulsed by the Marines, this attack is considered the closest the Germans would ever get to the French capital. Halting the Germans was a remarkable feat when you consider the significant failure in coordination between 2d Battalion, 5th Regiment, around Les Mares Farm, and 1st Battalion, 6th Regiment, on the right of 2d Battalion, 5th Regiment's position near Champillon. The German attack directed against the farm failed to take advantage of this gap between the units to the east of the farm. The failure of the 4 June attack at the farm is generally acknowledged as the high-water mark of the German offensive.

Directions to Stand 3 (Hill 142 View) (travel duration: 5 minutes): continue north on the Les Mares Farm road in the direction of Bussiares. At the first intersection, continue straight across the road and park somewhere in the farm service area. Exit your vehicle and walk to the southern

---

[23] Williams (1887–1918) was wounded during the battalion's fighting in Belleau Wood on 12 June 1918. He died from his wounds while at the battalion aid station in Lucy-le-Bocage later that day. Posthumously promoted to major, he received multiple Silver Stars for his actions at Belleau Wood.

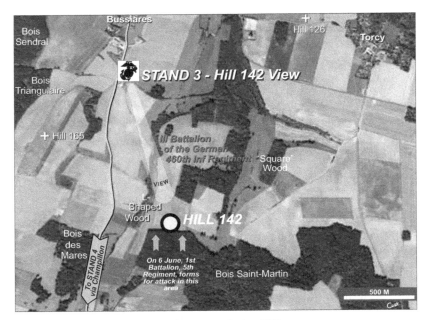

Figure 14. Stand 3 overlook to Hill 142.
Le Portail IGN, courtesy of LtCol R. L. "Bill" Cody, USMC (Ret)

edge. Look southeast with the road on your right (figure 14).

Stand 3. Hill 142 View
(travel duration: 15 minutes)

To orient the view, the road runs generally north-south. Looking to the southeast, you can see the edge of the woods from which the Marines of the 1st Battalion, 5th Regiment, attacked early on 6 June. The use of the term *Hill 142* is really a misnomer as there is no geographic elevation of that height. The French maps of the period contained a point marked "Côte 142" near the tree line that appears to have been a kind of property reference point. Hill 142 is in reality a long finger of terrain sloping downward to the north. Whatever its origin, as the only notation on the maps available at the time, it was used as a description of the area through which this preliminary attack was to take place. The 1st Battalion, 5th Regiment's two lead companies, 49th and 67th, attacked abreast, moving north out of the tree line and encountering stiff opposition in the woods to their front and due east from your position. In addition, the 67th Company, the closest to this stand, was struck in the open field by automatic fire from the area directly to your south, or the right of the road. Private Joseph M. Baker's actions reflect an individual act of bravery as he was awarded the Distinguished Service Cross and Navy Cross during this murderous assault. The citation reads:

> *The President of the United States of America takes pleasure in presenting the Navy Cross to Private Joseph M. Baker, U.S. Marine Corps, for extraordinary heroism while serving with the 67th Company, 5th Regiment (Marines), 2d Division, A.E.F. in action at Belleau Woods, France, 6 June 1918. When his platoon was suffering casualties from the fire of a hidden machine-gun, Private Baker exposed himself to a heavy fire to take up a position on the flank of the enemy gun. He attacked and killed the gunner by rifle fire and then rushed the gun, killing the crew with his bayonet.*

By midday, despite heavy casualties, the Marines controlled the entire wooded area to the east, due in large measure to the timely arrival of the rest of the battalion and Army engineers. Late in the afternoon, Gunnery Sergeant Ernest A. Janson (a.k.a. Charles F. Hoffman) led a counterattack against enemy machine gunners on the eastern edge of the final posi-

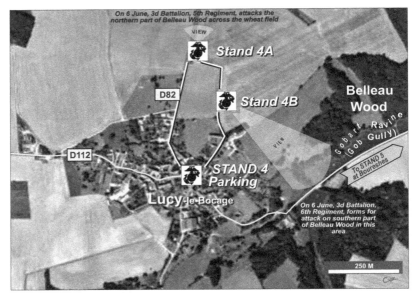

Figure 15. Stands 4A and 4B outside Lucy-le-Bocage.
Le Portail IGN, courtesy of LtCol R. L. "Bill" Cody, USMC (Ret)

tion for which he would later be awarded a Medal of Honor.[24]

Directions to Stand 4 (Lucy-le-Bocage) (travel duration: 10 minutes): return to your vehicle and proceed south from the viewing area, passing through the village of Champillon. At the road junction, turn left (east) to return to Lucy-le-Bocage and park in the village center (figure 15).

---

[24] GySgt Janson (1878-1930) enlisted in the Marine Corps on 14 June 1910 under the alias Charles F. Hoffman, having previously deserted from the Army. Appointed a gunnery sergeant, a temporary warrant for the duration of the war, on 1 July 1917, he served honorably with the 49th Company, 5th Regiment, in its various activities and on 6 June 1918, was severely wounded in action. He was reinstated to his wartime rank of gunnery sergeant in July 1926 and retired the following month. He was advanced one grade to sergeant major on 31 August 1926 and placed on the retired list on 30 September 1926.

Stand 4. Lucy-le-Bocage–Wheat Field Battlefield (travel duration: 45 minutes)

This village served as the focal point of the efforts of the 4th Brigade in and around the village with battalion aid stations and supply dumps. As you park in the village center, you can see the village church. Unfortunately, it is generally closed to the public. Although the structure was severely damaged during the battle, the crucifix above the altar survived intact, much to the amazement of all who saw it (figure 16). Those wishing to visit the church must contact the Saint-Crépin les Vignes's parish in advance, which is responsible for the church, by phone (+33(0)3.23.83.25.77) or by email (paroisse.sclv@orange.fr) to make arrangements.

You will be leaving the vehicle here and walking about 1 kilometer round-trip to Stand 4A. Walk north out of the village (Route D82) and turn right at the first unimproved farm road at the crest of the ridge. Continue on this farm road for approximately 75 meters and orient yourself north by facing left.

Stand 4A. The Wheat Field (travel duration: 15 minutes)

To your front and right lies Belleau Wood. To your left is Bois Saint-Martin (in 1918, it was called Bois de Champillon). This forest served as the assembly area for both brigade assaults into the woods: the first on 6 June and the second on 11 June.

The first attack, an assault by 3d Battalion, 5th Regiment, went from your left to right front; and the poorly coordinated assault of 3d Battalion, 6th Regiment, was directly behind to your right rear into the southwest corner of the woods. The German defensive positions in Belleau Wood were at the tactical edge of the forest, meaning a yard or two inside the tree line from which you can easily observe,

Figure 16. The Lucy-le-Bocage church crucifix survived the battle.
U.S. Army Signal Corps

and was dominated by automatic weapons. As described by Lieutenant General Merwin H. Silverthorn (1896–1985) in 1973, who was a sergeant in 3d Battalion, 5th Regiment, they started the attack late and left the woods in "trench warfare formation." This was the "only formation we knew, which consisted of four waves with . . . all waves holding their rifles at . . . high port [with fixed bayonets], not even aiming or firing."

There was 75 meters between the first and second wave of platoons with the third and fourth waves 150 meters farther behind. Once the German firing began, out of the 52 men in Silverthorn's platoon, only 6 made it through the first 75 meters. The general and other survivors found safety in a portion of the field that provided sufficient cover. The attack failed and the field before you was littered with casualties. If you look directly in front of your position, you will note the field is not exactly flat and there is a low area that dips to the right. It is likely that this area saved many Marines from 3d Battalion, 5th Regiment, such as Silverthorn, as they were able to find cover from the enemy fire and enter the edge of the woods to mingle with the left-most units of 3d Battalion, 6th Regiment.

Stand 4A is also the location of 2d Battalion, 5th Regiment's attack on 11 June, with artillery preparation beginning at 0300. Lieutenant Colonel Frederic Wise's battalion fought its way into the woods with better results than on 6 June, due in large measure to better intelligence and artillery preparation.

One final note about this area: during the night of 13–14 June, an artillery attack occurred south of this location against 2d Battalion, 6th Regiment, as it attempted to relieve the 5th Regiment's 2d Battalion. While preparing to deploy from the woods south of Lucy-le-Bocage, the battalion suffered many gas casualties. During this barrage, Gunnery Sergeant Fred Stockham, 96th Company, saved the life of one his Marines at the cost of his own by giving the Marine his gas mask as he carried him to the battalion aid station behind the village of Lucy-le-Bocage.[25]

Directions to Stand 4B: continue on the farm road as it turns to the right (south) and returns to the village, stopping about halfway from the farm buildings. Look east and note the terrain sloping to the south. Just beyond that point and to the south runs the Lucy-Bouresches road.

---

[25] GySgt Stockham (1881–1918) enlisted in the Marine Corps in 1903. In September 1917, after volunteering for service in France, he joined the 96th Company, 6th Regiment, at Quantico, VA. He was awarded the Medal of Honor for his actions during the Battle of Belleau Wood, France, on the night of 13–14 June 1918, when he exposed himself to mustard gas to give his own gas mask to a wounded comrade. He died from the effects of the gas on 22 June 1918 and was posthumously awarded the nation's highest decoration on 21 December 1939, due in large measure to the efforts of then-Col Clifton Cates, who was a lieutenant in the company at Belleau Wood, and fellow Marine turned prominent politician, Barak T. Mattingly, one of the men he saved.

Stand 4B. Southeast Corner
(travel duration: 15 minutes)

The left flank of 3d Battalion, 6th Regiment's attack covered this area. This battalion fared better overall, as the Marines were closer to the woods and did not have to assault over a wide-open space. However, due to the sloping terrain and heavy fire from the woods itself, they were channeled down the slope and into the creek bed along the Lucy-Bouresches road. This terrain feature known as Gob Gully was used as an avenue of approach for Marines going into and out of the woods during the battle. Thus, the battalion was unable to penetrate the woods very far and struggled to move along the Lucy-Bouresches road to capture Bouresches. Later that day, Major Thomas Holcomb's 2d Battalion, 6th Regiment, was directed to take Bouresches. Near this location, the 6th Regiment commander, Colonel Albertus Catlin, who was responsible for command of the attack, was severely wounded as he tried to observe the ongoing assault. With his medical evacuation, the deputy regimental commander some distance in the rear, Lieutenant Colonel Harry Lee, assumed command of the assault, leading to additional coordination problems throughout the day.

Directions to Stand 5 (Bouresches) (travel duration: 10 minutes): return to your vehicle in Lucy-le-Bocage and drive via the road to the east toward Bouresches. As you exit the village, you will notice Gob Gully to your right that runs from behind the village of Lucy into Belleau Wood to your left. Due to German artillery fire directed at roads and intersections on their maps, troops were encouraged to approach the front lines from rear areas and limit their movements to other avenues of approach.

As you draw near Bouresches, note the high ground in the woods to your left, giving you some idea of the tasks

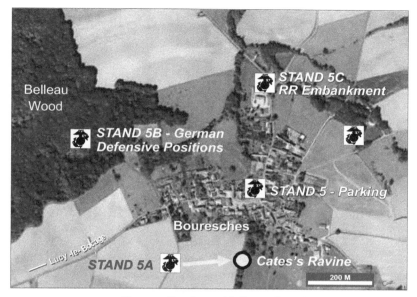

Figure 17. Stand 5 outside Bouresches.
Le Portail IGN, courtesy of LtCol R. L. "Bill" Cody, USMC (Ret)

required of assaulting troops, especially the Marines of 1st Battalion, 6th Regiment, who were moving from your right to the left across the road on 10 June. Gob Gully is located where the fields meet Belleau Wood and provided cover to the Marines who made it that far. As you approach the village of Bouresches, the farmland to your right is the area through which the 2d Battalion, 6th Regiment, attacked into the village (figure 17). Navy dentist Lieutenant (JG) Weedon Osborne died in that field on 6 June 1918, attempting to save the 96th Company's commander, Captain Donald Duncan.

Marines in Bouresches were resupplied via the road from Lucy-le-Bocage by trucks running the gauntlet of enemy fire from Belleau Wood and the railroad embankment outside Bouresches for several days. One particularly heroic attempt was organized by the legendary Sergeant Major John H. Quick of the 6th Regiment late on 6 June for which

Figure 18. Bouresches church, ca. 1918.
Marine Corps History Division

he, and the other participating Marines, were awarded Navy Crosses.[26]

Stand 5. Bouresches
(travel duration: 60 minutes)

Stop and park in the village center, note the church to the east at the intersection of the Belleau-Bouresches and Lucy-Vaux roads (figure 18). To the northwest lies Belleau Wood. The Germans held the village with their main line of resistance being the railroad embankment outside the village to the north to be visited later. Late on the afternoon of 6 June 1918, the 2d Battalion, 6th Regiment, attacked the village across the fields south of the Lucy-Bouresches road, while the regiment's 3d Battalion attempted to secure the

---

[26] SgtMaj Quick (1870–1922) was the 6th Regiment's sergeant major who had been awarded the Medal of Honor for his actions at Guantánamo Bay, Cuba, in 1898. He served during the rest of the war until he returned to the United States in October 1918.

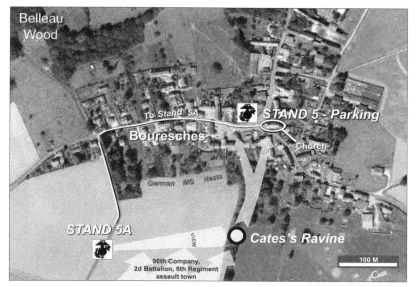

Figure 19. Stand 5A view toward Cates's Ravine.
Le Portail IGN, courtesy of LtCol R. L. "Bill" Cody, USMC (Ret)

southwest edge of Belleau Wood. Standing in the village center and looking toward the church, you can see the culvert on the right that contains the ravine (or creek bed) by which Second Lieutenant Clifton Cates and Marines from the 96th Company, 2d Battalion, 6th Regiment, advanced into the village, eventually driving the German defenders out.

Directions to Stand 5A (Cates's Ravine) (travel duration: 10 minutes): from the village center, walk out of the village on the road back toward Lucy-le-Bocage. Approximately 300 meters from the church, just before the end of the village, turn left (south) and follow the farm trail between a hedge on the left and a house on the right leading into the open field. Stop about 250 meters up the slope and turn and face the village (figure 19).

Stand 5A. Cates's Ravine
(travel duration: 15 minutes)

You can now see the village and Belleau Wood (to your left across the road to the north) from the perspective of the Marines in 1918. Across this field, the 96th Company attacked late in the afternoon of 6 June 1918. Assembled in the woods to the south, they struck with the objective of taking Bouresches. In this vicinity, Lieutenant (JG) Osborne was killed as he attempted to save the life of Captain Duncan.

Somewhere in this open field, Cates was knocked unconscious by a blow to the head from a glancing enemy projectile. When he recovered shortly thereafter, he noticed Marines moving toward the shelter of the ravine (to your right) that provided safe access to the village. This ravine to the east is labeled as Cates's Ravine in figure 19. There was a bitter struggle for the village through the night of 6 June, but eventually the 96th Company's Marines were reinforced by the battalion's 79th Company and soldiers from the Army's 2d Engineer Regiment. Major Randolph T. Zane, commanding the 79th Company, assumed command of all forces in the village and successfully repulsed counterattacks for the next several days. He was awarded a Distinguished Cross and the Navy Cross for his leadership during this phase of the battle.

Stand 5B. Supplemental–German Defensive Positions
(travel duration: 60 minutes)

Some areas in the southeast corner of Belleau Wood offer an excellent perspective on German defensive positions and some appreciation for the terrain (figure 20). However, this excursion requires time, effort, and good walking shoes. The round-trip from the road is about .5 kilometers and takes about an hour.

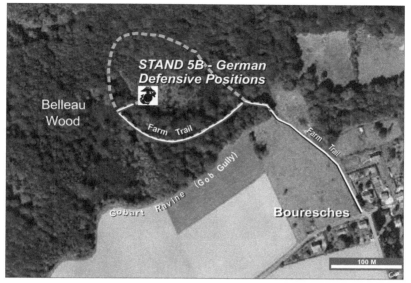

Figure 20. Stand 5B German positions in Belleau Wood.
Le Portail IGN, courtesy of LtCol R. L. "Bill" Cody, USMC (Ret)

Directions to Stand 5B (German defensive positions) (travel duration: 15 minutes): return to the hard-surface road and walk directly across it onto the farm trail leading to the southern edge of Belleau Wood. About 200 meters from the road, you will cross Gob Gully. Once across the ravine, follow the trail to the left at the fork and note how the terrain rises as you proceed farther into the woods. Follow the trail as it curves right. Proceed for about 200 meters into the woods from the trail fork. Note where the embankment on the right eventually is level with the trail. At that point, turn to the right and walk into the woods approximately 50 meters. Continue forward, inclining to the southwest until you reach the top of this high ground (figure 21). You will find several fighting positions among some large rocks and boulders that appear naturally oriented to defend the position.

Figure 21. Fighting positions in the southeast corner of Belleau Wood.
Courtesy of the author

This area was manned by German defenders against the attacks by 1st Battalion, 6th Regiment, beginning on 10 June.

From this location, it is easy to appreciate the dilemma of the attacking Marines, as these positions are situated on the high ground covering the southern access to the woods. Also, the nature of the terrain and dense forest highlights the challenges faced by the defenders in coordinating with adjacent units. Field Marshal Erwin Rommel, a German lieutenant and combat veteran of the war, highlighted the problems for both sides with forest fighting in his memoir, *Infantry Attacks* (1935):

> *One sees nothing of the enemy. The bullets strike with a loud crash against trees and branches, innumerable ricochets fill the air, and it is hard to tell the direction of the enemy fire. It is difficult to maintain direction and contact in the front line; the commander can control only the men closest to him, permitting the remaining troops to get out of hand. Digging shelters in a woods [sic] is difficult because of roots. The position of the front line becomes*

Figure 22. Rue du Lt J. G. Osborne.
Courtesy of the author

untenable when . . . one's own troops open fire from the
rear, for the front line is caught between two lines of fire.

This hazard in dense terrain helps to explain Major Wise's (2d Battalion, 5th Regiment) confusion on 11 June. In addition, it contributed to the poor coordination between the German defenders on 10–11 June that enabled the destruction of the *2d Battalion, 40th Fusiliers*. Retrace your route and return to the village center (travel duration: 30 minutes).

Directions to Stand 5C (Bouresches railroad embankment) *(travel duration: 30 minutes)*: proceed north to the outskirts of the village (by foot or vehicle). Across the street from the church on your left, you will notice a street sign on the building—Rue de Lieutenant J. G. Osborne—which is named for the Navy dentist who was awarded the Medal of Honor. Figure 22 is a photo of another street sign at the end of the village near the railroad embankment. The signs show a mis-

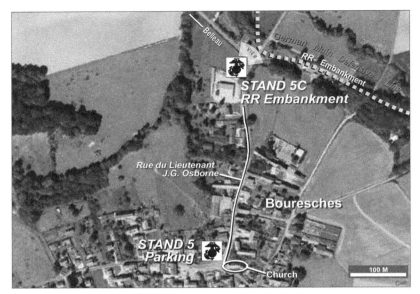

Figure 23. Stand 5C Bouresches railroad embankment.
Le Portail IGN, courtesy of LtCol R. L. "Bill" Cody, USMC (Ret)

understanding in Osborne's initials, mistaking the letters "J. G." in his rank (i.e., lieutenant, junior grade) as the initials for his name. His full name was Weedon E. Osborne. If you continue north to the next intersection (approximately 400 meters from village center), you will see the remnants of the railroad embankment and bridge to the north that crossed the road in 1918.

Stand 5C. Bouresches Railroad Embankment
(travel duration: 10 minutes)
This built-up embankment was the main German line of resistance and offered the defenders excellent fields of fire into both the village and the southern edge of Belleau Wood (figures 23 and 24 a/b). An objective of the Marine brigade, the Germans held it throughout the battle.

Figure 24a. Bouresches railroad embankment, ca. 1918.
Courtesy of Marc André Dubout

Figure 24b. Bouresches railroad embankment, 2018.
Courtesy of Gilles Lagin

Directions to Stand 6 (Belleau Wood memorial park) (travel duration: 15 minutes): return to your vehicle and proceed back to Lucy-le-Bocage. In the village center, turn right (north) and drive out of the village (Route D82). At the first hard-surface road intersection, turn right and drive through the Belleau Wood memorial park gate and continue until you

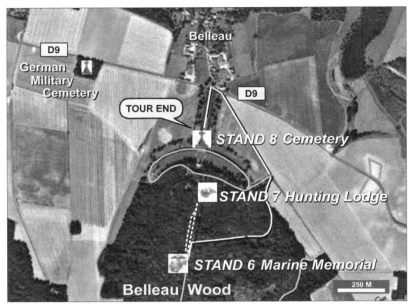

Figure 25. Stands 6, 7, and 8 outside of Belleau.
Le Portail IGN, courtesy of LtCol R. L. "Bill" Cody, USMC (Ret)

reach the center of the park at the Marine monument with the artillery displays. Park where space is available (figure 25).

Stand 6. Belleau Wood Memorial Park
(travel duration: 15 minutes)

You are now in the center of the northern half of Belleau Wood. The grounds no longer contain the dense undergrowth present in 1918, as the area is maintained now by the American Battle Monuments Commission as a memorial to the Americans who fought here. The monument and flagpole were erected in 1955. The then-Commandant of the Marine Corps, General Lemuel Shepherd, who distinguished himself during the battle as a second lieutenant in 2d Battalion, 5th Regiment, officiated at the ceremony. As noted in the cemetery brochure, the bronze bas-relief monument was designed and dedicated in 1955 by Felix de Weldon, who

Figure 26. The Marine Memorial, Belleau Wood.
Courtesy of the author

also designed the Marine Corps War Memorial (a.k.a. Iwo Jima Memorial) in Arlington, Virginia (figure 26).

This part of the woods was the center of the German defense as the battle progressed through mid-June, with the Marines in a desperate close-combat struggle. Survivors noted that no one on either side could expose themselves without being shot. Due to the nature of the German defense, using machine guns to support each other in the dense growth, exhausted Marine units had to be withdrawn beginning on 13 June. The U.S. Army's 7th Infantry Regiment relieved the Marines during 17–22 June but failed to

Figure 27. The hunting lodge after the battle.
Marine Corps History Division

expel the enemy. The German units fared little better as a depleted *461st Regiment* finally withdrew. As a result, German headquarters decided to abandon efforts to retake lost ground and concentrated on holding what they had.

Directions to Stand 7 (Hunting lodge/pavilion) (travel duration: 5 minutes): walk north from the park center on the gravel road. As you approach a gated wire fence at the edge of the cemetery grounds, you will see on your right the remains of the hunting lodge of the family who once owned Belleau Wood (figure 27). German accounts referred to it as the pavilion.

Stand 7. Hunting Lodge/Pavilion
(travel duration: 15 minutes)
In this area, the final operations of the battle took place. The hunting lodge or pavilion was the focal point of the German positions throughout the battle. If the gate is locked, you can visit this area from inside the cemetery grounds at the conclusion of the itinerary.

During the evening of 22 June, Major Maurice Shearer, commanding the now replenished 3d Battalion, 5th Regiment, was knocked out of the battle on 6 June, planned for the final assault. The next day, the battalion recovered ground lost by the 7th Regiment but made very little progress against the German's *347th Regiment*. On 24 June, General Bundy, the division commander, chaired a meeting with the leadership of the Marine brigade to include the regimental and battalion commanders and division artillery commander. To break the stalemate, the group decided to direct the division artillery to pulverize the northern portion of the woods with a heavy artillery attack in the early hours of 25 June. With the Marines withdrawing south sufficiently to avoid friendly fire, the 2d Division artillery regiment with support from French batteries fired on this area for 14 hours beginning at 0300. Surprisingly, the renewed Marine attack encountered some German survivors who continued to stubbornly defend their positions. However, slowly but surely, German resistance collapsed and units fell back to positions on the Torcy-Belleau road. By dawn on 26 June, Marines held Belleau Wood.

If you have additional time within the Belleau Wood Park, you can refer to the cemetery's Belleau Wood Trail Map brochure prepared for the 2018 WWI Centennial Commemoration and available at the visitor's building. It contains a walking trail map of interesting locations and terrain features in Belleau Wood and a brief synopsis of the battle (figure 28).

Directions to Stand 8 (Aisne-Marne American Cemetery) (travel duration: 15 minutes): return to your vehicle and drive north through the park, following the hard-surface road to the right down the hill. At the intersection after exiting the woods, turn left toward Belleau, noting the cemetery to your

Figure 28. Aisne-Marne American Cemetery entrance.
Courtesy of the author

left. Turn left on Route D9 and then take an immediate left to the cemetery grounds. Proceed toward the buildings and use the parking lot on the right.

Stand 8. Aisne-Marne American Cemetery (travel duration: time varies)

At this point during the final hours of the battle, the retreating Germans were pushed back through this area to the village of Belleau. Visitors can now devote time to visiting the cemetery, the Visitor Center, and Memorial Chapel. Dedicated in 1937, the cemetery covers 42.5 acres with 2,289 gravesites. Medal of Honor recipient Navy Lieutenant (JG) Weedon Osborne is buried about halfway down to your left as you face the chapel. His gravesite is distinguished by the gold lettering on the cross. In the chapel, the names of 1,060 Americans missing in action are listed.

At the far left edge of the cemetery, a lone gravesite (plot A, row 13, grave 91) can be found of an unknown American whose remains were discovered in a ravine north of Hill

142 by a local farmer in 1988. Breaking historic precedent, the cemetery was reopened for a formal military funeral conducted by the Marine Corps on 5 November 1988 at the request of then-Commandant General Alfred M. Gray Jr., as it was believed the remains may have been that of a Marine. Unfortunately, there was no evidence to determine either identity or Service. Records show Army soldiers served in the 4th Brigade, and Army units served in the area after the Marines departed. However, Gray felt strongly that it should be the Marine Corps' responsibility to conduct the burial if this young man died near Belleau Wood.

Supplemental Visits in the Village of Belleau (travel duration: 30 minutes)

The well-known Devil Dog Fountain is located in the stables of the old château in the village of Belleau north of the cemetery. The fountain sits on privately owned property and is not open to the public. If you wish to visit the fountain, you must make inquiries with the cemetery staff or someone at the village of Belleau museum (across the street from the stables) who can provide access as the gate to the stables is kept locked (figure 29).

If you visit the fountain, you may want to visit the Belleau village cemetery just across the Clignon Brook north of the château's stables. Exit the stables, turn left, and proceed across the creek. The cemetery lies directly ahead. It contains the grave of the last American soldier to die in Belleau Wood. On the morning of 2 April 1928, members of the Aisne-Marne American Cemetery staff discovered the body of Ernest Stricker, who had committed suicide near the hunting lodge the previous evening. A private first class in an Army engineer unit during the war, Stricker was honorably discharged in 1919, but appears to have suffered from post-traumatic stress-disorder and other medical problems

Figure 29. Devil Dog Fountain.
Official U.S. Marine Corps photo, courtesy of Cpl Daniel Wulz

in the years following the war. He left a note in a Paris hotel room stating that his health was failing and he could not go on. He wished to be buried in France among his "comrades in arms." As the military cemetery was closed to burials, the villagers of Belleau offered to give him an honored place. Thus, on 5 April 1928, Stricker was buried with full military honors in the village cemetery (figure 30). When the Aisne-Marne American Cemetery staff place American flags at the gravesites in the military cemetery each year to commemorate Veterans and Memorial Day, they also place one at Private First Class Stricker's grave.[27]

Summary
Stand 8 concludes the field guide. It is our hope that you have now gained some appreciation of the momentous bat-

---

[27] PFC Stricker (1891–1928) is listed as ISOB, which indicates isolated burial; in this instance, ISOB refers to a burial site that is decorated on U.S. holidays but rests outside of one of the ABMC cemeteries.

Figure 30. Ernest Stricker funeral, ca. 1928.
National Archives and Records Administration

tle waged here in 1918 and of the sacrifice and heroism of the soldiers, sailors, and Marines from another century. What is the legacy of those valiant Marines? As General Charles C. Krulak, 31st Commandant of the Marine Corps, wrote in the *Marine Corps Gazette* in 1998:

> *At Belleau Wood, the Marine Corps discovered that warfare had changed, and we had failed to adapt to those changes. The 4th Brigade paid the price in blood. Those who survived never forgot that lesson, and they vowed that the Corps would never again be caught unprepared. They became the innovators, risk takers, and visionaries who championed amphibious assault in the 1920s, close air support in the 1930s, and vertical envelopment in the 1950s. They were the architects [who] built the force-in-readiness that we are the proud stewards of today.*

Semper Fidelis!

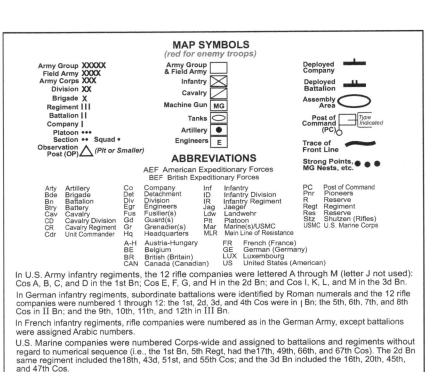

MAP SYMBOLS
(red for enemy troops)

In U.S. Army infantry regiments, the 12 rifle companies were lettered A through M (letter J not used): Cos A, B, C, and D in the 1st Bn; Cos E, F, G, and H in the 2d Bn; and Cos I, K, L, and M in the 3d Bn.

In German infantry regiments, subordinate battalions were identified by Roman numerals and the 12 rifle companies were numbered 1 through 12: the 1st, 2d, 3d, and 4th Cos were in I Bn; the 5th, 6th, 7th, and 8th Cos in II Bn; and the 9th, 10th, 11th, and 12th in III Bn.

In French infantry regiments, rifle companies were numbered as in the German Army, except battalions were assigned Arabic numbers.

U.S. Marine companies were numbered Corps-wide and assigned to battalions and regiments without regard to numerical sequence (i.e., the 1st Bn, 5th Regt, had the 17th, 49th, 66th, and 67th Cos). The 2d Bn same regiment included the 18th, 43d, 51st, and 55th Cos; and the 3d Bn included the 16th, 20th, 45th, and 47th Cos.

EXAMPLES OF COMBINING SYMBOLS AND ABBREVIATIONS

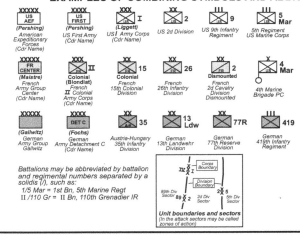

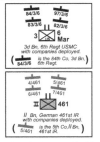

BIBLIOGRAPHY

The National Archives, College Park, Maryland
Records Group 117, "Records of the American Battlefield Mon-
uments Commission," RG 117.4.2, correspondence with
officers of the 2d Division, AEF.
Records Group 120, "Records of the American Expeditionary
Forces," 2d Division files.
Records Group 127, "Records of the United States Marine Corps."

Personal Papers Collection, Archives Branch,
Marine Corps History Division
Bellamy, David. Diary.
Blake, Robert. Memoir.
Cates, Clifton B.
Cumming, Samuel C., My Last Day in World War I.
Duermit, J. W. My Diary.
Elliot, N. Diary.
Erskine, Graves B.
Goudenough, Frank E. Memoir.
Mills, C. B. Memoir.
Montague, Robert M. Memoir.
Snare, Carl D., Sr. How I Won the Big War.
Stenbeck, Raymond Howard.
Thomas, Gerald C. Memoir.

Oral History Interviews and Transcripts, Oral History Section, Marine Corps History Division

Cates, Clifton B.

Erskine, Graves B.

Hermle, Leo D.

Krulewitch, Melvin L.

Noble, Alfred H.

Paradis, Don V.

Shepherd, Lemuel C., Jr.

Silverthorn, Merwin H.

Published Books and Unit Histories

American Armies and Battlefields in Europe: A History, Guide and Reference Book. Washington, DC: American Battle Monuments Commission, 1938.

    The best reference tool to date on AEF operations.

Asprey, Robert B. *At Belleau Wood.* New York: G. P. Putnam's Sons, 1965.

    A classic work of military history, this campaign history is indispensable to any study of Belleau Wood.

Bellamy, Capt David. *History of the Third Battalion, Sixth Regiment, U.S. Marines.* Hillsdale, MI: Akers, MacRitchie & Hurlbut, 1919.

Brannen, Carl Andrew. *Over There: A Marine in the Great War.* Preface and annotation by Rolfe L. Hillman Jr. and Peter F. Owen. College Station: Texas A&M University Press, 1996.

Cates, Gen Clifton B., USMC. *History of the 96th Company.* Washington, DC: Headquarters Marine Corps, 1935.

Catlin, BGen Albertus W., and Walter A. Dyer. *"With the Help of God and a Few Marines."* New York: Doubleday, Page, 1919.

Clark, George B. *Devil Dogs: Fighting Marines of World War I.* Novato, CA: Presidio Press, 1999.

_____, ed. *Major Awards to U.S. Marines in World War One.* Pike, NH: Brass Hat, 1992.

    These award citations provide interesting details on combat operations.

_____. *Their Time in Hell: The 4th Marine Brigade at Belleau Wood, June 1918.* Pike, NH: Brass Hat, 1996.

_____. *Retreat, Hell! We Just Got Here!: A Brief Biographical*

Sketch of Lloyd W. Williams. Pike, NH: Brass Hat, 1994.

Cochrane, Rexmond C. *Gas Warfare at Belleau Wood, June 1918*. Washington, DC: U.S. Army Chemical Corps Historical Office, 1957. Reprinted by Books Express Publishing, 2011.

Cron, Hermann. *Imperial German Army, 1914–18: Organisation, Structure, Orders of Battle*. Translated by C. F. Colton. Solihull, UK: Helion, 2002.

Derby, LtCol Richard, Medical Corps (USA). *"Wade in, Sanitary?": The Story of a Division Surgeon in France*. New York: G. P. Putnam's Sons, 1919.

Donaldson, George H., and W. Jenkins. *Seventy-eighth Company, Sixth Marines, Second Division Army of Operations*. Neuwied, Germany, 1919.

Drury, Clifford M. *The History of the Chaplain Corps, United States Navy*, vol. 1, *1778–1939*, NAVPERS 15807. Washington, DC: Government Printing Office, 1948.

Falls, Cyril. *The Great War*. New York: Capricorn Books, 1959.

Field, Cpl Harry B., and Sgt Henry G. James. *Over the Top with the 18th Company, 5th Regiment, U.S. Marines: A History*. No publisher, 1919. Reprinted by Pike, NH: Brass Hat, undated.

Fosten, D. S. V., and R. J. Marrion. *The German Army, 1914–18*. London: Osprey, 1978.

Gibbons, Floyd. *"And They Thought We Wouldn't Fight."* New York: George H. Doran Co., 1918.

Gillett, Mary C. *The Army Medical Department, 1917–1941*. Washington, DC: Center of Military History, United States Army, 2009.

Gordon, George, V. *Leathernecks and Doughboys*. Chicago: George V. Gordon, 1927. Reprinted by Pike, NH: Brass Hat, 1996.
Gordon was an Army officer serving with 16th Company, 3d Battalion, 5th Regiment.

Gudmundsson, Bruce I. *Stormtroop Tactics: Innovation in the German Army, 1914–1918*. Westport, CT: Praeger, 1989.

Gulberg, Martin Gus. *A War Diary*. Chicago: Drake Press, 1927.

Handbook of the German Army in War, April 1918. Nashville, TN: Battery Press, 1996.

Harbord, Gen James G. USA. *The American Army in France, 1917–1919*. Boston, MA: Little, Brown, 1936.

_____. *Leaves from a War Diary*. New York: Dodd, Mead, 1925.

Hemrick, Levi E. *Once A Marine*. New York: Carlton Press, 1968.

Hildebrand, Karl-Friedrich, and Christian Zweng. *Die Ritter des Ordens Pour le mérite des I. Weltkriegs* [The Knights of the Order Pour le mérite of the First World War]. Biblio-Verlag: Osnabrück, 1999.

History of the Second Battalion, Fifth Marines, U.S. Marines. Neuwied, Germany: privately printed, 1919. Reprinted by Brass Hat, undated.

History of the Sixth Machine Gun Battalion, Fourth Brigade, U.S. Marines, Second Division: And Its Participation in the Great War. Neufeld on the Rhine, Germany: 1919. Reprinted by Brass Hat, 1993.

History of the Sixth Regiment United States Marines. Tientsin, China: Tientsin Press, 1928.

Hopper, James. *Medals of Honor*. New York: John Day, 1929.

Jackson, Warren R. *His Time in Hell: A Texas Marine in France, The World War I Memoir of Warren R. Jackson*. Edited by George B. Clark. Novato, CA: Presidio Press, 2001.

Kean, Robert Winthrop. *Dear Marraine, 1917–1919*. Privately printed, 1969.

Keegan, John. *The First World War*. New York: Alfred A. Knopf, 1999.

Krulewitch, Melvin L. *Now that You Mention It*. New York: Quadrangle, 1973.

Lejeune, MajGen John A. *The Reminiscences of a Marine*. Philadelphia, PA: Dorrance, 1930.

Livesey, Anthony. *Great Battles of World War I*. London: Greenwich Editions, 1996.

Lynch, Col Charles, Col Joseph H. Ford, and LtCol Frank W. Weed. *The Medical Department of the United States Army in the World War*, vol. VIII, *Field Operations*. Washington, DC: Government Printing Office, 1925.

MacGillivray, George C., and George C. Clark, eds. *A History of the 80th Company, Sixth Marines*. Pike, NH: Brass Hat, undated.

Mason, Charles Field. *A Complete Handbook for the Hospital Corps of the U.S. Army and Navy and State Military Forces*. New York: William Wood, 1906.

McClellan, Maj Edwin N. *The United States Marine Corps in the*

World War. Washington, DC: Historical Branch, G-3 Division, Headquarters Marine Corps, 1920, revised 2014.

McQuain, Thomas Bryan. *To the Front and Back: A West Virginia Marine Fights World War I.* Berwyn Heights, MD: Heritage Books, 2005.

Millet, Allan R. *In Many a Strife: General Gerald C. Thomas and the U.S. Marine Corps, 1917–1956.* Annapolis: Naval Institute Press, 1993.

Owen, Peter F. *To the Limit of Endurance: A Battalion of Marines in the Great War.* College Station: Texas A&M University Press, 2007.

Rendinell, Cpl Joseph E., and George Pattullo. *One Man's War: The Diary of a Leatherneck.* New York: J. H. Sears, 1928.

Scarbrough, Byron. *They Called Us Devil Dogs.* Self-published, Lulu Press, 2005.

Schlacten des Weltkrieges. Oldenburg/Berlin: Gerhard Stalling, 1930 (in German).
    This is the German Reich Archives account of the Great War published between 1921 and 1933 in 35 volumes.

Simmons, BGen Edwin H., and Col Joseph Alexander. *Through the Wheat: The U.S. Marines in World War I.* Annapolis: Naval Institute Press, 2008.

Spaulding, Col Oliver Lyman, and Col John Womack Wright. *The Second Division, American Expeditionary Force in France, 1917–1919.* New York: Hillman Press, 1937. Reprinted by Battery Press, 1989.

Strott, George G. *History of Medical Personnel of the United States Navy, Sixth Regiment, Marine Corps, American Expeditionary Forces in World War, 1917–1918.* Leutesdorf am Rhein: privately printed, 1918. Reprinted by Brass Hat, 1993.

_____. *The Medical Department of the United States Navy with the Army and Marine Corps in France in World War I.* Washington, DC: Bureau of Medicine and Surgery, Navy Department, 1947. Reprinted by Battery Press, 2005.

Suskind, Richard. *Do You Want to Live Forever!* New York: Bantam Books, 1964.

_____. *The Battle of Belleau Wood: The Marines Stand Fast.* London: Macmillan, 1969.

Thomason, Capt John W., Jr. *Fix Bayonets!* Washington, DC: Marine Corps Association, 1925.

_____. *The United States Army Second Division Northwest of Chateau-Thierry in World War I.* Edited by George B. Clark. Jefferson, NC: McFarland, 2006.

Toland, John. *No Man's Land, 1918: The Last Year of the Great War.* New York: Anchor Books, 1980.

The Two Battles of the Marne: The Stories of Marshal Joffre, General von Ludendorff, Marshal Foch, Crown Prince Wilhelm. New York: Cosmopolitan Book, 1927.

Unruh, MajGen A. D. von. "The German Side." Sidney Rogerson. *The Last of the Ebb: The Battle of the Aisne, 1918.* S. Yorkshire, UK: Frontline Books, 2007. First published by Arthur Barker, London, 1937.

Venzon, Anne Cipriano. *From Whaleboats to Amphibious Warfare: Lt. Gen. "Howling Mad" Smith and the U.S. Marine Corps.* Westport, CT: Praeger, 2003.

War Department, Office of the Adjutant General. *Histories of Two Hundred and Fifty-One Divisions of the German Army which Participated in the War (1914–1918).* War Department Document No. 905. Washington, DC: Government Printing Office, 1920. Reprinted by London Stamp Exchange, 1989.

_____. *Manual for Noncommissioned Officers and Privates of Infantry of the Army of the United States.* New York: Military Publishing, 1917.

_____. *Records of the Second Division (Regular).* 9 volumes. Washington, DC: Second Division Historical Section, Army War College, 1927.

_____. *Translations of War Diaries of German Units Opposed to the Second Division (Regular).* 9 volumes. Washington, DC: Second Division Historical Section, Army War College, 1930–1935.

Williams, Ralph L. *The Luck of a Buck.* Madison, WI: Fitchburg Press, 1985.

Wise, Col Frederic May. *A Marine Tells It to You: As Told to Meigs O. Frost.* New York: J. H. Sears, 1929. Reprinted by the Marine Corps Association, 1981.

Woodward, David R. *The American Army and the First World War.* Cambridge, UK: Cambridge University Press, 2014.

Periodicals

Anderson, Col William T. "Devil Dogs in Olive Drab: The 2d Engineers at Belleau Wood." *Army History*, no. 58 (Spring 2003): 20–29.

_____. "Guest of the Kaiser: A Private's Tale." *Fortitudine* 33, no. 2 (April 2008): 18–20.

_____. "Gunnery Sergeant Fred W. Stockham: Contempt of Personal Danger." *Leatherneck*, June 2008, 38.

_____. "To Get Back in the Fight: Major Randolph Scott Zane, USMC 1887–1918." *Leatherneck*, September 2012, 24.
A biography of Maj Randolph Zane, commander of 79th Company, 2d Battalion, 6th Regiment, who defended Bouresches.

Barnett, B. J. "Blood and Wheat." *Leatherneck*, December 1942, 16–17, 54–59.

Cornelius, Cdr George, USN (Ret). ". . . P'lice Up a Little Brass," U.S. Naval Institute *Proceedings*, November 1997, 45–47.
An account of battle as told by Pvt Hal P. Spencer, 1st Battalion, 6th Regiment, in 1970.

Daugherty, Leo J., III. "And They Thought We Wouldn't Fight." *Leatherneck*, June 1998, 30–35.

_____. "General Clifton Cates, USMC at Belleau Wood June 1918." *Marine Corps Gazette* (June 1998): 35–36.

Dieckmann, Edward A., Sr. "Dan Daly, Reluctant Hero." *Marine Corps Gazette* 44, no. 11 (November 1960): 22–27.

Hacala, Mark T. "The U.S. Navy Hospital Corps: A Century of Tradition, Valor, and Sacrifice." *Navy Medicine*, May–June 1998.

Hancock, Marianne. "My Father Was a Hero." U.S. Naval Institute *Proceedings* 104, no. 11 (November 1978): 89–93.

Homsher, David C. "Securing the Flanks at Belleau Wood." *Military History* 14, no. 2 (June 1997): 54–60.

McClellan, Maj Edwin N. "The Aisne-Marne Offensive." *Marine Corps Gazette* 6, no. 1 (March 1921): 66–84.

_____. "The Aisne-Marne Offensive." *Marine Corps Gazette* 6, no. 2 (June 1921): 188–227.

_____. "Capture of Hill 142, Battle of Belleau Wood, and Capture of Bouresches." *Marine Corps Gazette* 5, no. 3 (September 1920): 277–313.

_____. "Capture of Hill 142, Battle of Belleau Wood, and Capture of Bouresches." *Marine Corps Gazette* 5, no. 4 (December 1920): 371–405.

_____. "Operations of the Fourth Brigade of Marines in the Aisne Defense." *Marine Corps Gazette* (June 1920): 182–215.

Nelson, Havelock D. "Return to France." *Leatherneck*, May 1941, 7–9.

_____. "Paris-Metz Road." *Leatherneck*, January 1940.

_____. "We Go In." *Leatherneck*, May 1940.

Michael, Cdr W. Howard, USN. "Pleasure and Pain of 1918." U.S. Naval Institute *Proceedings* 60, no. 382 (December 1934): 1705–12.

Otto, LtCol Ernst (Imperial German Army). "The Battles for the Possession of Belleau Woods, June 1918." U.S. Naval Institute *Proceedings* 54, no. 11 (November 1928): 941–62.

Patton, W. Kenneth. "Navy Medical Corps–Its Gestation, Birth and Baptism." *Navy Medical Newsletter* 55, February 1970, 3–5.

Rendinell, J. E., and George Pattullo. "Memorandum from the Director: Remembering General Shepherd." *Fortitudine* 20, no. 2 (Fall 1990): 3–11.

_____. "One Man's War." *Saturday Evening Post*, 16 July 1927, 3–5, 141–42, 145, 148–50, 152.

_____. "One Man's Battle." *Saturday Evening Post*, 13 August 1927, 8–9, 66, 71–72.

Simmons, BGen Edwin H. "The Great War Crucible." *Naval History* 19, no. 6 (December 2005): 16–23.

U.S. Navy. "The History of the Corps–Medical Corps." *All Hands* no. 705 (October 1975): 28–30.

Waller, Maj L. W. T., Jr. "Machine Guns of the Fourth Brigade." *Marine Corps Gazette* 5, no. 1 (March 1920).

Wilmeth, 1stLt J. D., USA. "Bois de la Brigade de Marine." *Marine Corps Gazette* 23, no. 1 (March 1939): 26–29, 58.

ABOUT THE AUTHOR

William T. Anderson retired from the Department of Defense in 2005 after more than 35 years of service. From 1987 to 2005, he served as a senior legal advisor at the Supreme Headquarters Allied Powers Europe, the operational military headquarters for the NATO. He attended Hampden-Sydney College in Virginia and later received a bachelor's degree in economics from American University. He holds a law degree from Washington and Lee University and a master's degree in political science from Georgetown University with a special emphasis on security studies. He was commissioned in the Marine Corps in 1969 and served as a judge advocate in both the 1st Marine Division and the 1st Marine Aircraft Wing at the conclusion of the Vietnam War. In 1980, Anderson became a civilian international attorney in the Department of the Navy in Washington, DC, until he was seconded by the Department of Defense to the NATO assignment. He retired as a colonel in the Marine Corps Reserve in 1999 following duty as deputy chief of staff, Marine Corps Forces, Europe. From 2009 to 2017, he served on the adjunct faculty, College of Distance Education and Training, Command and Staff College, Marine Corps University at Quantico.

CPSIA information can be obtained
at www.ICGtesting.com
Printed in the USA
BVHW031740220820
586901BV00031B/1601